BY THE SAME AUTHOR

Especially Spaniels

The Book of Stillmeadow
Stillmeadow Kitchen
Flower Arranging for the American Home
(in collaboration with Ruth Fisher)
Especially Father

BY THE SAME AUTHOR

☆

Long Tails and Short
The Book of Stillmeadow
Stillmeadow Kitchen
Flower Arranging for the American Home
(in collaboration with Ruth Kistner)
Especially Father

Especially Spaniels

by
GLADYS TABER

WITH PHOTOGRAPHS BY
JILL
(Eleanor S. Mayer)

Macrae · Smith · Company
PHILADELPHIA

COPYRIGHT, 1945, 1949, GLADYS TABER

A new and enlarged edition

TWELFTH PRINTING

498

Manufactured in the United States of America

THIS BOOK BELONGS TO

Dark Star, who wanted a place in the country
and changed our lives entirely;
Ripplemark, who was the most steadfast
and noblest companion;
Quicksilver, who is "Sister" to everybody,
the sunniest and most merry;
Windy Dawn, gentleman;
Saxon, Chief Petty Officer in the Navy, Dogs for
Defense, but amiable in the kitchen;
Spring Night, the tempestuous daughter of Star;
Sweet Clover, whose heart has love enough
for the whole world;
Snow-In-Summer, as simple and open as a field
daisy.

AND IT BELONGS TO

Silver Wings and Melody and Hildegarde, who
look at life with love and laughter, being young
and gay.

AND IT BELONGS TO

Musketeer and Static and Donna who were with
us such a little time, but are always in our hearts.

AND IT BELONGS TO

Dark Honey, the golden, remote and dreamy one,
who has edited this little book herself.

Especially Spaniels

☆ ☆ ☆ ☆ ☆ | ☆ ☆ ☆ ☆ ☆

My first experience in the care of young animals came at an early age. On my way home from school one afternoon, I took a short cut through a back alley. Walking dreamily along, swinging my book bag, I stumbled over a brown paper sack. The sack was humping up and down in an odd manner, and making noises.

It was full of newborn kittens.

Clutching the sack firmly against my flat chest, I raced home and began a battle against nature which has gone on in one form or another in my life ever since. I lost this first round, because the kittens had been too long in the cold alley, but my fierce efforts kept the strongest alive far beyond reason.

Later I experimented housebreaking two white rabbits named Romeo and Juliet. They were both males. They were as white as polar snow and their eyes were the color of burning opals, and I couldn't bear to keep them in their hutch. Besides, the bulldog next door was constantly coming over to sit on top of the hutch, and it made them uneasy.

I made, I must admit, only fair progress in this

venture. My rabbits *would* forget. They just didn't give their whole minds to housebreaking. But they followed me all over the house like puppies, stopping now and then to thump loudly the way rabbits do. And in spite of their mistakes, I was a happy child because I was the only one in town with house rabbits!

My third venture was in breeding. This was in the bird field. To the casual observer, a canary bird seems a rather modest little fellow, with a clean quiet eye. Cheerful by nature. Rather a Pollyanna as to temperament. Acting on this theory, my hard-pressed family allowed me to have three canaries, two Mammas and one Papa. I had a nice cage for them, with fancy grillwork in green and gold.

My three canaries, in this happy home, put on a fight that would have done credit to Madison Square Garden. Feathers flew through the embattled air, sifted all over the house. The cage rocked on its standard. Now and then, one canary would fall on the floor of the cage, eyes closed, wings raw. But before I could take it out, it would rise again and with a scream advance to the battle.

I got a second cage and moved two canaries to that. It was like one of those horrid mathematical puzzles because I never found a combination of any two that would be satisfied. The man who tried to get the goose and fox and grain over the river in a rowboat had my deepest sympathy.

Finally, I had a third cage, three birds, three cages. They sat hunched up in their solitary state, glaring unhappily through the bars at one another, and now and then throwing seeds out. Once they got to throwing sulphur grains and all the solid silver in the dining room turned black as ink.

Naturally enough, there were no babies. So I gave away the most agitated female and started over. Several times the tea strainer nest had an egg in it, and the little Mamma worked herself to skin and bone tearing up papers and tossing them on the floor. The eggs, however, always mysteriously vanished, and no birds sang.

Came the day when I was offered for high school graduation whatever I most desired. I could have a lovely diamond ring! Or a new fur coat. Or—what did I want?

I wanted a dog. Nothing but a dog.

Timothy was an Irish setter, more precious than a barrel of diamonds and wearing his own fur coat, deep and lustrous and red as maples in Autumn. Timmie lived fourteen years, but looking back on it, I am surprised that he did. For the only available advice in those days on the care of dogs was given to me by a cow-doctor. We *called* him the cow-doctor. He prescribed a diet for my darling which consisted chiefly of scotch oatmeal boiled in a big kettle until it was a gelid mass, and with meat chunks stirred in.

On this fare, naturally, Timmie had recurrent

and bad attacks of skin disease so his hair fell off in great patches. The doctor had no idea of what caused this curious ailment, but prescribed sulphur and lard. Timmie used to wear a kind of shift made of old underwear with the lard and sulphur spread under it. You could smell him from a long way off. The hair came in again, probably because he ate so much from my own plate, but then he would have another attack. Some dogs do, the doctor said sagely.

All of this was in the pre-vitamin era.

Much later, after a brief sally with tropical fish, the dream of my life became a reality and a mellowed fate presented me with cocker spaniels.

Stillmeadow kennels became a fact.

☆ ☆ ☆ ☆ ☆ 2 ☆ ☆ ☆ ☆ ☆

Most of what I have learned about spaniels came the hard way, through experiment and experience. There always seemed to be things happening to dogs that are not taken up by the dog manuals. However, after years of working with cockers, I have evolved a technique in dog raising and care which has some good features.

As an amateur expert, I like to pass on whatever I have learned to help other dog-minded people.

Particularly I feel sympathy for the dog owner who does not live next door to a dog hospital staffed with experts. A good veterinarian is a gift without price. He can safeguard your dog through life, tell you how to feed and when and what, what sort of soap is best, whether the puppy has worms or swallowed a theater ticket. He inoculates your pet for distemper, the prime murderer of dogdom. He has X-ray, operating equipment, and every new aid to modern science. In fact, the devotion I feel toward our own veterinarian is such that the family predicts that if I ever met with an accident, I would murmur as they picked me up, "take me to the Dog Hospital".

This is a controversial subject, I realize. For example, a year or so ago, I took a fatally ill cocker to the hospital. There he received blood tests, intravenous treatments, special sedatives for pain, day and night checks on heart beat. The fluoroscope evidenced that no foreign object in his poor little insides was causing extra trouble. When he failed to get well, the doctor said gently, "there was nothing left undone." And though I was a sodden wreck, I felt that every human resource had been mobilized in the battle and it helped me.

A week later a lady wrote me, "Why did you take your dog to a hospital to die? Don't you know veterinarians always kill them? If you really loved him, you wouldn't have sent him off to be killed!"

These are the people who don't call the doctor in time for their children. I have little patience with them.

But the sad truth is that there aren't enough good veterinarians to go around. Hundreds, perhaps thousands of people in little faraway farms or remote villages, just can't get a good doctor! They have to do the best they can on their own.

There are also, alack and alas, still many inefficient veterinarians, a kind of backwash from the days of my cow-doctor for Timothy. A friend of mine once took her puppy to be de-fleaed. She paid three dollars and placidly came home with her darling, only to find him scratching like a flock of nervous hens. When I examined him, the fleas were having old-home week.

"But I had paid three dollars! He can't have fleas!" my friend cried.

The dog and I thought differently. And I got rid of the fleas for him.

If you are fortunate enough to live near a good veterinarian, consult him for emergencies, by all means. The rest of the time, may you find help in these pages for the problems that rise when a dog takes over your heart and hearth.

3

What kind of dog shall I buy? This is the first question you ask.

Buy the best dog you can afford.

A mongrel, contrary to legend, is not better than a purebred dog. The pleasant fiction has long been abroad that a mongrel, picked up from a garbage can, is smarter, stronger, more lovable than a pedigreed puppy whose father and mother were born with silver spoons in their mouths. There will be times when the picture of that mythical happy mongrel chasing equally robust alley cats and dining lustily on old potato peels; there will be times when this picture, I say, will make you gnash your teeth as you pour tomato juice down the reluctant throat of your own daughter of champions.

But ask this mongrel where the rest of his family is and he will sadly tell you he is the sole flower left on the family tree. He is the last of the litter, too tough to die, but he is a pig in a poke as far as his future is concerned.

Any breeder of livestock from cows to kangaroos will tell you that no scrub stock compares well with thoroughbred. Those big plump eggs you pay too much for come from hens that live with one eye on the correct mash and the other on their inherited laying characteristics.

Sometimes you can't help having a mongrel. An enormous black dog once adopted a cousin of mine. He simply came up on the porch and barked, and when she opened the door, he came in and put his suitcase on the sofa. He resembled, in appearance, something out of one of the grimmer Russian plays, but he had a heart of gold. His tail had been sold him by the yard, cheap, and he had a G.I. haircut. He could eat right round the clock, and he was most helpful with the housework, whisking vases from tables, piling up rugs and knocking lamps over. Though he was as big as a pony, he never got over believing he could sit in her lap, if she had helped a little.

He was a diamond in the rough, and everyone has known other excellent mongrels, too. But I still say, if you have an opportunity to pick out a dog, select one that brings his papers with him in his wallet.

For a dog that has the benefit of years of careful line breeding by experienced breeders and has had scientific care before he takes you home with him, has all the trump cards in the deck. He is beautiful, intelligent, he has quality. He will, within the limits of his understanding, never let his ancestors down!

The correct way to purchase such a dog is to get him at a reliable kennel. Or better still, from a breeder who raises a few litters a year and does it by hand, so to speak. Individually raised puppies are like home-bred children compared to institutionally-raised youngsters.

It always amazes me to find people who seem normally intelligent who will dash out and pick up a puppy from a pet shop they happen to pass by or a roadside stand that is on the way to the lake or from a push-cart vendor. They will swallow the old one about the papers having been burned, or the one about the records being lost. Or the really imaginative tale about the sire being owned by one man and the dam another and the feud that grew up so neither breeder would relinquish any papers attesting the mating. This one, palmed off in many variations, has undeniable charm as a fable.

Some of my friends have spent good money on a pedigreed puppy that the breeder said had championship background, but the papers were temporarily mislaid and would be forwarded later. Later never came. When the dog turned out to be a cross between a piano and a corner cupboard in appearance, they were terribly surprised.

The protection against chicanery is available to anyone. It is the protection of the American Kennel Club, the national organization devoted exclusively to the purebred dog. This clearing house for dogdom keeps on file the registration of the purebred dogs of all the standard breeds.

If the papers for your puppy have been burned or lost or given to the waste-paper salvage by mistake, the Kennel Club will still have the record of the complete transaction. Also, the sire and dam will have their own A. K. C. numbers, right in those files. More, you can check back on the parentage of their great-grandparents and find out the numbers of their parents!

Moreover, both breeders at the time of mating, attest to the breeding of the sire and dam, and nearly always the owner of the dam will register the entire litter at birth. The litter registration number comes right home with you when you carry your darling away in the new pink baby blanket.

Then, if you are sensible, you will obtain an individual registration for your dog by writing to the American Kennel Club, 221 Fourth Avenue, New York City, New York. You fill out the required blank and forward it with the necessary fee. At this writing, the fee is a dollar provided the litter has been registered within ninety days of birth and the whole litter is being registered at the same time. Otherwise the fee is two dollars.

The Kennel Club blanks are very confusing, but if you set your teeth and do your best, you may only have them returned a couple of times to be corrected. It is worth it, whether you ever show your dog or have puppies.

☆ ☆ ☆ ☆ ☆ 4 ☆ ☆ ☆ ☆ ☆

The breed of dog you choose depends entirely on your own personality. Every breed has its own charm, its own assets and, I say frankly, its own liabilities. Even dogs are not entirely perfect. For instance, if you want a dog that can lick his weight in wildcats, a cocker is a poor choice. Cockers are wonderful hunting dogs, and some of them are fine watchdogs and some of them like to bite milkmen, but by and large, a cocker is a non-belligerent. If you want a dog whose hat is always in the ring, don't buy a cocker. The first bulldog you meet may send your puppy flying to your arms. Or if he mixes with the bulldog, the bulldog will make mincemeat of him.

If you want an independent life-of-its-own kind of dog, walk softly past the kennel where cocker puppies sit always facing the back door of the house. If you don't want your puppy to tell you all, and confide every waking thought and be under your feet at every step, try a sturdy wise little Scottie or a dashing wire-hair.

When I limit my talk to cockers, it does not mean that I fail to appreciate Great Danes. It means only that cockers have been a part of my life, night and day and day and night for so many years that I am intimate with them to the nth degree. Most of the care of cockers is similar to the care of any breed. The general treatment is the same, subject of course to variations because of size.

If you choose a cocker above other breeds, you should know just what you are letting yourself in for. The typical cocker has one aim in life and it is a major aim. His aim is to BE WITH YOU EVERY SINGLE MOMENT. His feeling for you is like a five-alarm fire. He doesn't care a penny about leading his own life, he only wishes to lead yours. If you are in the attic sorting old letters, he wishes to sort old letters in the attic. Much as he enjoys hunting rabbits and woodchucks, he will give it up in a minute to sort old letters in the attic. If you are trying to lie down and rest, he feels a sudden need to rest, and rest on the same couch.

He probably will not actually leap in the bathtub with you, but he may rest his paws on the edge and watch you. And you may as well give up any closed-door policy that you have had. Cockers are allergic to doors closed between you and them.

When cruel fate takes you away from your cocker, there will be the most passionate welcome when you return, even if you have only stepped out for five minutes to buy some stamps. There are people who would be bored by all this devotion. Cockers are not for them.

But if you don't get tired of being told how wonderful you are, how perfect, how all desirable, a cocker puppy is your dish. As I write this, seven cockers are helping edit the manuscript. With a whole house to roam in, all seven are trying to squeeze between me and the typewriter, just to let me know THEY STILL CARE!

This leading characteristic of spaniels is primarily responsible for their wonderful adaptability. They will live in town, in the country, in a penthouse or a walk-up. They will hunt happily all day long or be satisfied with a brief walk around a few lamp posts. They are excellent dogs for invalids or shut-ins or for busy people who cannot spend hours pounding the pavements to exercise the puppy.

They demand little, except your love.

They are also happy dogs. They have a neat sense of humor, and perpetual-motion tails. Their eyes may look large and wistful, but their madly whirling tails belie them. Intelligent, impulsive, often very sensitive, they meet life eagerly.

In the field, they make splendid hunting companions. Even with no training at all, they will retrieve the neighbor's chickens and do very well with rabbits in the garden.

They are more sensitive to sound than many breeds. A good thunderclap sends some cockers under the bed. They have no poise with the roar of fire engines or the racket of riveting machines. Even a hissing radiator can throw them in a state. But I don't like noise myself, so I am able to respect this phobia.

Almost any cocker can be taught to be kind to cats. They are not killers as a rule, though they may be chasers. And a houseful of cats and cockers is easily managed, whereas some of the other breeds just can't admit cats to their league of nations.

Spaniels have been called the "kennel angels". Possibly that sums it up as well as anything. At any rate, if you choose a cocker, he will give you the love that passeth understanding until death do you part, and for all I know, afterward too.

☆ ☆ ☆ ☆ ☆ 5 ☆ ☆ ☆ ☆ ☆

There is no use lying awake nights wondering whether to get a male or a female. In any given litter rolling around a pen, there will be one particular puppy who will see you as you come up. This puppy will detach himself or herself from the mob and bounce on you, saying happily, "Here, this is me! I've been waiting for you long enough!"

You may have decided that a female is too much nuisance, so you pay your money and the puppy takes her choice and you go proudly off with a female. Or you want nothing *but* a female because the last dog you knew was a female and was much smarter than any male, and you get home with a puppy you name Buster or Rover.

Whatever you have, the general public will assume the puppy is a male. I am often stopped on the street as Star takes me out. Star is a great-grandmother and as feminine a piece of sugar and spice as ever lived.

"Oh, look at him! Isn't he cute?" someone invariably says.

Or when Honey takes a maternal stroll between nursing times for the puppies, someone always exclaims, "There! Look at that sweet little fellow! How old is he?"

I wonder why boats are always referred to as feminine and cats are usually referred to as "she", but dogs are always masculine.

There are, however, as a matter of cold fact, as many female dogs as there are male.

Theoretically I prefer females. If I had only one dog, which Heaven prevent, it would be a female. But I am glad I don't have to choose.

By and large, I think females are quicker and more adaptable, and if you live in the city, easier to take out. A female will take a nice walk with you in a practically straight line, but a male makes you weave back and forth and round about indefinitely. When I walk in the city, I like to walk on the path in the park, not simply tour from fire hydrant to fire hydrant.

There is absolutely no point in buying a female if you are going to have her spayed. Get a male instead. Plenty of eminent authorities will rise and tell me spaying does not affect the dog if it is done early enough and not too early and by a good veterinarian. But I have never known a breeder who wouldn't agree with me. Spaying does change something intangible in the whole being of the dog, quite aside from the extra weight and slowness she acquires and the fact that she ages faster. You may hold the weight down by keeping her on K rations most of the time, but you can't compensate for the glandular changes that must take place. And, incidentally, it doesn't really improve a puppy to have a major operation early in life with the nervous shock and the hospital experience. Generally speaking, you can't improve on nature and her plans any more than you can rewrite Shakespeare.

Many people have their females spayed because of a superstitious fear of the time she is "in season". It is true that about twice a year, the female will be in heat. The interval varies for the individual somewhat.

During these periods, contrary to general belief, you are still able to live in your house, entertain friends and influence people much as usual. To come right out and call a spade a spade, there will be very few mopping-up processes for you to attend to. Many fearful souls expect to undergo as much mess as an operation clean-up.

If you put a clean bathtowel on the best satin chair which Sweetie-pie sits on, or, if you are so lax as to actually allow her to sleep on your bed, lay an old folded blanket-throw across the taffeta bedspread, you will be pleasantly surprised at how well you and Sweetie-pie carry this thing off.

Once in awhile you may have a bit of touching-up to do with a dab of clean cold water. Now is this actually such a fearful and horrendous struggle? On the contrary, if you aren't careful, Sweetie-pie may be half through her heat before you know it.

But the neighbor's dog will know it and let you know it if he has a chance. This is the time to keep her away from males unless you have serious intentions and a marriage license in your dog kit. But actual mating will not take place during the entire season. Keep in mind that the bitch will breed only during the latter of the period and this may save you many heartaches when you want a litter of soft and earnest-eyed babies.

The first symptom is a very slight colorless discharge which gradually becomes redder until the ninth or tenth day when it begins to taper off. From fourteen to twenty-one days for the whole season is a good general estimate. Some bitches will breed sooner than others, but the twelfth to fourteenth day is average. There will be an enlargement of the external tissues which will diminish as the breeding period draws to a close.

Many owners have been bitterly disappointed when they anticipated a litter of puppies and the mating was unsuccessful.

In pre-war days, people often drove to Stillmeadow with their darlings in their arms. They would say ecstatically, "We want some puppies! Some puppies exactly like Sandra!" When I asked how long Sandra had been in season, they might say vaguely, "Oh, I don't know—I haven't any idea—"

If they had been as wise as Sandra, they would have known. Nine times out of ten, it would be too late or too early. It is a good plan to begin to count the time when you realize that the bitch is in heat as already part way through it. Allow a margin of two or three days when you didn't know about her state.

There are symptoms other than the physical to watch for also. There is a kind of moonlight-and-roses expression in those dreamy eyes, an extra affectionate attitude, and presently the would-be mother will wash her paws, wash your hands, wash the sofa cover, wash her toys. If she is a born mother, like Honey, she will wash the skin off anything she can.

This to me, is the beginning of the greatest miracle on earth. In the secret depths of her being, the magnificent, ancient forces of creation are awake already. Your little pampered darling is preparing to bring new life into the old tired world. She is now more than just your pet, she is a part of destiny.

Now if you have chosen a male and believe sex will have no concern with him, you are mistaken. The male may have wandering fits, and he may howl incessantly at times when the moon is just right. He may have shivering fits, an upset stomach. If you are in the country he may disappear and drive you frantic with worry. If you are in

Central Park, he will drag you like a blown leaf all over the rocks and through the rills.

Of course this isn't his fault. He can't help having a love-life. If all dogs were males, he might stay quietly in his armchair with his pipe and book, but there are still females in the world. He himself had a mother.

And the worst of it is, he may get these spells any time, whereas a female has only two seasons a year. If you don't want him run over, you will have to watch him carefully when he is in a dancing mood. He may be kidnaped, or get in a bad brawl with another gay blade. Or the neighbors may complain to the police.

For the howling, give him aspirin, one tablet for a medium-sized dog, half a tablet for a young dog. And if you have access to the lady who is breaking his warm little heart, spray her quarters with a mixture of citronella and lemon extract, half and half. Mix the two well and use a flit gun or small plant spray. When I have a number of bitches in season, I spray the male also. This may be unorthodox, I don't know, but it helps. This is not a preventative of breeding, however, but will aid and comfort the nerves. Both human and canine.

Breeding your male once will not calm him down for life. You may as well admit that the great law of all living creatures is to reproduce, to carry the precious life-force from generation to generation, and when you thwart this law, some difficulties are bound to result. I believe, from my own observation, that if it can be managed, any dog is better for being bred at least once.

But you won't blight your dog forever by not breeding him. He will sublimate as much as possible and try hard to keep his mind on the higher things of life.

Females will take it out on whatever is at hand. I have seen females mothering everything from old golf balls to tin cans. And we once went through a desperate period when a little particolor bitch, too young to have her own, kept moving in and trying to adopt a nice lively litter belonging to Snow-In-Summer. If the door was ever left ajar, Silver Wings was in the whelping box in a state of manic excitement and joy. And no matter how many times Snow found her there and tore her to pieces, she only crept away and waited for another chance.

That litter was raised in such an uproar that I thought they would all have complexes. On the contrary, they turned out to love everybody and fear nothing. Possibly two mothers would benefit most children.

☆ ☆ ☆ ☆ ☆  ☆ ☆ ☆ ☆ ☆

WHAT is the best age to buy a dog? Between eight and twelve weeks is the ideal time for a puppy to leave his birthplace and fare forth to conquer the world.

Some people adopt the attitude that if they get a dog two or three years old, they won't have to bother to raise it. That is much like adopting a college graduate for a child, to save going through measles and teething.

The mature dog has developed loyalties and habits, his enchanting puppy days are gone, and you yourself have not helped him develop into the exact image of your dreams. He may be housebroken and save your rugs, he may walk on the leash like a gentleman, but the chances are that as he trots staidly along, his heart is in the highlands.

Furthermore, if you are offered a perfectly trained dog of two or three years old, there is generally some good reason why the owner wants to get rid of him. There may be a catch in it somewhere. Better be sure.

A puppy is more fun. A cocker puppy at eight

32

COCKER SPANIEL PUPPIES (Two weeks old)

IT'S A LONG WAY DOWN! (Three weeks old)

SUPPER IS SERVED (Thirty-five days old)

CHAMPION NONQUIT NIGHT FLYER

weeks is really something to broadcast over a coast-to-coast hook-up. Sturdy little body romping toward you, morsel of tail whirling madly, soft deep ears lolloping, limpid eager eyes—and a personality that for keenness, teachability and loyalty cannot be surpassed, here is a prize worth having. When I see such a puppy, I always wonder what the breeders buy that's half so precious as the stuff they sell! But the answer is simple. They go out and buy dog food for more spaniels!

As to color, the dog under the coat is more important than the hue of the coat. The best body coat for a cocker is smooth, but there should be plenty of feathers on the legs, and the ears should have a good deep wavy texture to the fur. Thin, stringy hair on the ears is a poor characteristic, though often natural in reds and blondes.

The eyes should be dark and round, but not bulging. In the light reds and parti-colors they may be brown but of "a shade not lighter than hazel" according to the American Spaniel Club. The nose should be black except for light dogs when it may be either brown or black.

The muzzle should be finely modeled, squarish, with well-formed skull. There should be plenty of lip. The ears should be low set. A common fault in poor cockers is a snipy muzzle or a pinched looking nose with high ears.

The back should be short, body compact, with firm muscular hindquarters and a straight front, well-boned. The neckline should be sloping, neck not thick and short. The feet should be round and firm, and should never turn in or out.

The mature cocker should weigh not under eighteen nor over twenty-eight pounds.

In the show ring, a perfect cocker is a beautiful sight, standing with alert, wide-awake attitude, bright and merry eye, strong compact body and lustrous coat.

"But I still can't tell a good cocker from a poor one," wailed a friend of mine, "so how do I know which to buy?"

True, you may not pick a winner, but even if you "want just a pet" you should try for a good puppy. Stand off and look at the whole group of cockers as if you were looking at them to measure the whole breed. Quality will show, even to an inexperienced eye.

Most of the lines are straight, the effect of the whole blocky. See if the ear is joined at about the level of the eye line. Even a baby puppy will show whether his ears are riding up like kites or swinging low like a gentleman cocker's.

If I were buying a Saluki or a Siberian Wolf Hound, about which I know nothing at all, I should go about it in this same way and I believe I should get a good dog, if not a champion. I would look at the whole group and get the feeling for it.

A reliable breeder will do his best to help you get what you want. However, even breeders are human, and what looks like a champion in the whelping box may "go off" in later years. I once sat at a dog show beside the greatest cocker breeder of all time, Mr. Herman Mellinthin. A woman marched into the ring leading the saddest little rag-bag cocker ever exposed to public view. The great breeder buried his head in his hands and moaned softly, "Here comes one of my mistakes! And what a mistake!"

An established breeder will give you a square deal as far as possible. But not for five dollars!

I have known women—and men too, for that matter—who would never think of beating down the price on a radio or a coat, but who seem to think when they approach the purchase of a dog, they must become Arab traders. They will try to beat you down five or ten dollars because they really "just want a pet". Or they say they have only so much to spend and then they want the potential champion in the litter and no other.

They may want a wormed, housebroken, leash-trained show prospect and they blandly offer you thirty dollars. Well, fun is fun, but the milk of human kindness in most breeders is rapidly curdled by an offer of about half the amount he has actually spent to raise that puppy.

From thirty-five to seventy-five is a reasonable price range, though the good puppies at thirty-five are scarce as raspberries in January. For five, ten and fifteen dollars you get a dog that has four legs and two ears, but you won't get a good cocker. You seldom buy real diamonds in a ten-cent store either.

A sound, well-bred puppy brought to salable age and properly fed has already cost the breeder more than twenty-five dollars in the simplest set-up. If the bitch was bred to an outside champion, the stud fee alone was fifty to seventy-five dollars. The pre-natal care is expensive and the diet of the brood matron is far from cheap. Years of experience and work have gone into the making of this puppy, as well as brains and patience. Even if the breeder earns his living by selling insurance, he cannot sell you a good puppy for five dollars.

I have known purchasers, too, who would refuse to pay forty dollars for a healthy, wormed, clean puppy, but would get a nice little bargain for ten dollars and at once spend fifty in bills at the veterinarian while Fido was inoculated, wormed, de-loused and nursed through everything from hookworm to distemper. Fido may never be really rugged, he may be subject to illness all his life, but they will seldom stop to realize that Fido was a poor prospect when they got him.

Curiously enough, it is usually people with very little extra money who will pay the asking price for a good puppy. They seem to know instinctively what a puppy is worth and they count out the dollar bills from a worn purse with no question.

They want a good dog and they get the best the breeder has. But the diamond-loaded dowager will often try to buy the pick of the litter at five dollars less.

7

I ONCE sold a charming red puppy to a woman who seemed rather fussy. As a matter of record, I almost refused to sell her the puppy.

"She will yell her head off for a night or two," I said doubtfully. "You will certainly have trouble."

The next day when the phone rang, I expected the worst.

"You were entirely wrong about my dog!" the woman said triumphantly, "she never uttered a sound all night long! She was perfectly wonderful!"

"Well," I said, "well, that's fine. Remarkable, too. They usually feel pretty homesick all alone the first few nights— I really thought— Did you have her in the kitchen?"

"Oh, no," she said brightly, "she slept in bed with George and me."

At the opposite end of the scale are the people who want their dogs to live and have their being entirely outside the house. If you can enjoy toasting your feet by a good fire while your cocker huddles in an unheated kennel, there isn't any law against it. You can always tell him to remember the Huskies at the North Pole and be thankful for his nice doghouse.

I knew one dog, however, that wouldn't have anything to do with his large and nicely painted house. His owner even got in with him to show him how dandy the whole idea was. Bruno just got right back outside and left his owner in sole possession of the kennel. If you think it's so wonderful, he seemed to say, it's all yours.

Wherever he sleeps, the place must be dry, cool, protected from draughts. A cellar floor is not the place to keep your dog. Even a rumpus room, if it is underground, is no place for your dog to spend half of his breathing hours. He should have a bed of his own, if he isn't going to take over part of yours. The bed should keep him from the floor and preferably should be covered with a soft and washable cover.

The graceful baskets on sale at department stores make very pretty beds, but some puppies like to eat wicker. Our own Sister once consumed half of a wicker bed during the quiet hours of the night. But Sister had an odd taste for linoleum, too, in her youth, and walnut arm rests and carpets.

A wooden box with a pad that can be cleaned is a satisfactory bed. A washable blanket spread over a favorite chair provides comfort. Corrugated cartons fall in the class with wicker baskets as highly indigestible. But whatever the bed, don't begin by tucking the baby in with heavy blankets every night. A very young puppy may need a baby blanket for a time, but too much wrapping up makes a dog very sensitive and subject to respiratory diseases. We find that puppies sleeping in a cool room are healthier than those sleeping by a hot radiator.

To house a number of dogs, a great outlay of money is not essential. A good barn or shed lined with insulating board and with sleeping benches along the wall makes a good kennel. We used a barn and an old brooder house, laying a wooden floor sloped to a drain, and building runs with fox fencing, using cedar posts cut from our own land. We stained and waxed the sleeping bunks, so that they are easily kept clean.

We experimented with various bedding material, washed burlap bags, old woven rag rugs, meadow hay, peatmoss and cedar shavings. Most bedding gets wet and holds the dampness. We settled on straw finally, since it stays dry and does not disintegrate as fast as hay, and is relatively easy to clean out. We buy it by the bale from a local feed store. I think it is warmer than shavings, and it is certainly easier to take care of since you may always use it around the rosebushes and in the strawberry bed when the dogs are through with it.

During the winter, a low steady heat may be

maintained in your kennel with a reliable small heater. Openings to the runs should have a piece of heavy carpet fastened over the top to cut off the wind and still allow the dogs free access. A windbreak made from an old packing box is a help for a north opening. This may not make the kennel look exactly like the Waldorf, but keeps the cold out.

We use an oil heater firmly set on a fireproof base. A coal heater is good, if you have any coal, and if you watch out for coal gas. Electric heaters are fine if you can get them. We tried a brooder heater once, but never got it under control and so we gave it away. It was the most maddening contraption I ever saw.

It is great fun to be tucked up in bed at midnight and begin to worry about the kennel heater. You reason with yourself for half an hour or so, and then you rise and pull on a coat over your pajamas and stick your slippered feet in galoshes and fare forth.

The scenery is beautiful at that hour, and the dogs are enchanted to see you. Surprise, surprise, they say leaping up and knocking your flashlight under the bunks. You turn the heater up, turn it down, kiss the boys and girls good night, go back and turn the heater up again. You can always take aspirin the next morning for that cold you caught wading in the deep snow in your nightclothes.

Summer or winter, the kennel house must be scrubbed faithfully and sprayed with disinfectant. The runs must be raked and disinfected also. We use the spray attachment on the vacuum cleaner. We sprinkle agricultural lime on the runs and water them down with a sprinkling can. Generally after a good work-out at these chores, some city friend will arrive and say, "But aren't you bored way out in the country with nothing to do all day?"

It may sound trite to mention the old business about keeping fresh cool water always in the drinking pan. Some dogs are smart enough to trail after you carrying their waterpan in their mouths, and I know dogs who will go to the sink and yell for water, but many dogs will just patiently hope for the best. The amount of water a dog takes varies greatly. Some cockers drink all day and some only sip after meals. Usually I can tell who is at the pan by the sound of lapping.

Deep bowls are best for spaniels. There is the small matter of their ears. Some people have been known to pin the ears up with a clothespin but few self-respecting cockers would permit this.

If your dog is going to run loose in the yard, an ordinary fence will not keep him at home. An earnest spaniel can do a major excavation job if there is a chicken on the other side of the fence to encourage industry on his part. A series of boards sunk in the ground along the fence line will control the digging, but be sure the boards are painted with creosote before they are buried, in order to prevent rot.

It is perfectly true that cockers are stay-at-homes as a rule. They are usually found exactly outside the door nearest to you, just waiting. But it isn't safe to count on their never running after a passing kitten, and there are still hit-and-run drivers. There are people also who will throw milk bottles at your darling when he digs up their tulip bulbs.

My first dog, the Irish setter, had the run of the town. But that was a long time ago and the town was small. Timmie had a regular beat like a policeman, going from cat to cat, with pauses at the houses of his best friends for doughnuts and chocolate cake and steak bones. This was the recommended snack for pets. If he stayed away too long, we used to phone around and find where he was visiting. Then he was brought to the telephone and his ear held to the receiver. We told him firmly to come right on home, Timmie.

Presently he would come, flying down the street, one eye still keen for an unwary tomcat. Once he went to the railroad station with a friend, and the friend was boarding the train for Chicago, and felt a little concerned that Timmie might board it also. So he called up from the phone booth and managed to squeeze Timmie inside and hoist him up high enough to listen to his master's voice summoning him home.

But this is the only dog I ever knew who was good at the telephone.

☆ ☆ ☆ ☆ ☆ 8 ☆ ☆ ☆ ☆ ☆

Then there is housebreaking.

Many otherwise intelligent men and women who are able to balance their checkbooks and work crossword puzzles and master gin rummy seem to lose any vestige of sense when they wish to housebreak that little Christmas puppy Aunt Nellie so unfortunately gave Junior. They don't use, to put it frankly, the little good sense God gave a goose.

I remember selling an exceptionally fine puppy to a woman with a college degree. The puppy was at an early age broken to newspapers, perfectly at home with either the New York *Times* or the *Herald-Tribune* and I explained this. The next week the woman phoned that the puppy was not in the least degree housebroken, I had misrepresented the affair, and he was making mistakes all over the house.

I said, "Where did you put down the newspapers?"

"Oh," she answered, "I haven't put down any papers for him anywhere!"

I restrained myself with difficulty from pulling

the telephone from the wall and hurling it in her direction.

Then there are the owners who belong to the lost-soul group. They believe an eight weeks old puppy should be as well behaved as a patriarch. They would hardly expect a human baby to ask to go to the bathroom at the age of six months, but they feel a puppy should know all the facts of life at birth. Why this is, I never know. In the presence of such people, I maintain a grim, Rock-of-Gibraltar kind of poise, but it is an effort.

The rules for housebreaking are simple and involve using only a modest amount of common sense, mixed with a soupçon of patience.

First you should find out the kind of life your puppy has led before you came into it. Puppies raised in big commercial kennels probably will not begin on newspapers. Home-raised puppies may have been using papers in their box behind the kitchen stove. We find that keeping the pen lined with papers facilitates early housebreaking to a marked degree.

Some puppies may be housebroken at two months but they are really child prodigies and ready to make their debut at Carnegie Hall. At about twelve weeks they may begin to get the idea.

A young puppy will have three or four bowel movements a day and perform the lesser business ten or twelve times. Anyone who has seen a baby's diapers on the line can accept this frequency with no argument. You may feel that your puppy just waits until the phone rings or you turn your back on him a minute to get the mail and then rushes to the best oriental rug.

There will be moments when you may feel it would be easier to close the house and move out to the barn with the dog. You will be ready to send him back to Santa Claus, express prepaid. And then his eyes will look up at you and his fat legs will begin bouncing and his earnest loving tongue will lap your shoe and you will forgive each other and start again. He will never tell you it is partly your fault that things aren't running smoothly. He won't say, well, you are the big brain around here, aren't you? Get the mastermind on this little problem and help me out.

You know he will need attention after every meal. Feed him in one place and directly the napkin is folded and put down, put him on his newspapers. A small space completely covered with papers is best; we use a child's play pen, or fence in a corner in the back kitchen. You may have a small downstairs bathroom or powder room you can spare for a bit. But keep him on the papers until he is through. Then pat him and love him and admire him extravagantly.

I know of nothing more smug than the face of a semi-housebroken puppy who is squatting in the middle of the editorial column and being admired for it. There is a kind of glow in his eyes, a look of pride. This time we really pulled it off, didn't we? he asks.

Now, don't go out for the day and leave him in the drawing room with his papers in the kitchen. He can't remember that well yet. At first let him run at will in the house only for half an hour after he has done his duty by you. The rest of the time, keep a quick eye on him. The first thing when he wakes up from a nap, he will need attention. The last thing at night, too. All right, that makes six times accounted for, if your puppy is very young.

There are still a few extra times. When he begins to circle like a pinwheel, move fast. Pick him up and get to the paper with no local stops. If he moves thoughtfully, nose down, to a far corner of the rug, that is your cue again.

If he does make an error, go easy on your rage. Of course you never make mistakes of any kind yourself, but try to imagine how you'd feel. Never, never rub his nose in the mess. This barbaric practice should have gone out with the Spanish Inquisition. Speak to him sharply and, if you must, spank him lightly on his offending rear with a folded newspaper. Then put him where he belongs.

The spot marked X should be immediately deodorized and disinfected. I have known dogs who were perfectly housebroken, but only to one corner of the livingroom rug where they had made their first little error. A puppy tends to establish his own habits and if he finds a familiar smell on the Saruk, he will use the place again. There are several very good liquids on the market which clean and disinfect and also keep the rug color from fading. If you have none of these, wash the spot with cold water first, then with a cloth squeezed from soapsuds or dipped in Energine or Carbona or some household fabric cleaner.

Some people try to housebreak puppies entirely to the great outdoors. I am a fanatic believer in newspaper breaking first. At the age of five months or so, you may gradually move outside. By then you won't have to spend your entire day opening and closing the door and leaping about the yard or dashing down the street.

If your puppy is originally broken to papers, he can always fall back on them in a pinch. I personally don't care much about staggering out to the street at three in the morning if Percival has eaten something too laxative in his supper.

Or suppose you don't get home when you should?

I have a friend who owns a perfectly trained wire-hair, the type who would rather die than lose his virtue. He was housebroken easily and early to the curb or the bonnie briar bush. But then came the day my friend got mixed up with the great hurricane of '38. She found herself and her faithful friend in a hotel room with the lower floors awash and no communication with the outside world. From six in the evening until ten or eleven the next morning, she couldn't, simply couldn't take him out! The story of that night would bring tears to a gremlin. In vain she spread papers down, in vain she explained and pleaded. All night long the poor suffering dog stood at the door of the room and cried upon deaf Heaven to heed his prayers. Valiant to the end, he held out, but at what a cost, I hesitate to think. And by morning she was ready to take him down if they both had to swim for it.

A dog who has been thoroughly grounded in the newspaper technique will always be able to read the headlines if he has to.

The first few weeks that your dog has you, he will establish his routine and yours. Patience and care at that time will set him up for life, and you too. You will have years and years of pure unadulterated joy if you begin successfully. Of course some puppies housetrain more easily than others. I have seen puppies that were practically fool-proof as soon as they were weaned. And the spectacle of a fat unsteady puppy teetering solemnly over to a pile of newspapers is something to fill the watcher with awe.

Then again, there are dogs like one of my own beautiful little black bitches.

She could sit up, and speak, and sneeze, and retrieve, and walk on the leash, and ride like a lady in the automobile while she was still in rompers. But every time she got within climbing distance of a bed, preferably a clean, newly-made bed, she scrabbled gleefully up and used the exact center for a bathroom of her own. We tried all the tricks. Her liquid intake was regulated, her walks were frequent and long, she was shut in and shut out, and spanked with the *World Telegram,* and cajoled and bribed.

Finally in desperation I went back to the kennel where her mother was bred. It just happened that a handler was there trimming some dogs for a show, and while I waited for the kennel owner to appear, I mentioned my problem to him.

He laid down his stripping comb and gave me a long thoughtful glance. "Yeah," he said, "yeah. That's Marguerite's pup all right. Marg was sold and brought back to the kennel a coupla times on account they never could housebreak her. Then I spent three years on her myself, but she never did get housebroken. You better give up."

This was sound advice, but there was a catch to it. We loved her. She was soft and round and blacker than satin and she had a way of lifting her head and looking right down to your heart and— oh, well, I took her home and began all over again.

We trained her.

In after years, she was the mother of dozens of beautiful intelligent puppies. The hereditary weakness was transmitted only occasionally, and those few who inherited housebreaking difficulties were loved to distraction by their owners for their charm and beauty and sweetness. But most of them were stable little citizens ready to work their way through school selling the *Saturday Evening Post*.

We suffered long with that little black cocker, but when I think of the dividends that came with the years, the struggle seems smaller than a pinpoint.

Then there is the dog who wishes to remain paper-broken and does not like the idea of going outside. We had one like that too. My beautiful golden Honey would go to market and go to the fruit store and go to the post office, happy and serene, and come home and rush for her papers. Again I went through all the tricks. Finally one afternoon I took her out around one o'clock simply determined to have it out once and for all.

We went around the block sixteen times. We went to the park. We went to Riverside Drive. We went up to Columbia. My feet felt like coal barges very low in the water and pulling against the current. My back ached. An hour passed, two hours passed. Three hours passed.

At the end of the day, with dusk hanging a dim curtain over the city, Honey gave me a look from her dark, dreamy eyes, and squatted down in front of a fire truck. Triumphant and exhausted, we wended our way home just in time to find the family phoning the police to put in a five state alarm to the Missing Persons Bureau. From that day forth, Honey could live in Buckingham Palace and never be out of place.

These are extreme cases, and I tell them so that when your puppy takes a week or so to get the idea of housetraining, you will have a little patience. Nine times out of ten, you and the puppy get together on this problem in short order.

You may have such good luck that your puppy never makes a mistake. Then the pay-off comes just as you have finished telling a dog hater how marvelous your new treasure is. Perfect, you say, simply perfect. Never makes a mistake. Never. At this point, your little darling will undoubtedly run over to the visitor and squat neatly at her feet making the mistake of a lifetime. The dog hater thereupon knows the truth is not in you, and you lose your faith in the essential justice of the universe.

Comes the day when your puppy can be trusted, however, even on a social call of long duration. He is at home in society. My black problem child traveled across the country with me many times, in and out of revolving doors and hotel rooms and dining rooms and behaved perfectly. And when you take your puppy with you, and he swings along beside you, eager-eyed and merry, and with perfect manners, you both know in your hearts that the game was worth the candle. In fact, there are few things in life that will reward you so richly for your effort as the brief time you spend in housebreaking your dog.

9

Nearly all breeders come in time to be fanatics about diet. And the first question the veterinarian asks as he picks up your ailing pet is, "What have you been feeding him?" He is apt to ask this in a severe tone, as if he knew the real trouble with you is that you are raising your dog on a diet of horseradish and maple syrup.

Some dog owners have just about this much sense, it is true. I knew a woman once who couldn't understand why her dog cried night and day and seemed very feeble. It turned out she had been feeding him a tablespoon of raw beef for a meal, and nothing else. She got this curious idea from the veterinarian who had prescribed this diet for a sick puppy, aged six weeks.

There are many misconceptions about diet for dogs, and this is not strange when you consider the odd beliefs often held about human diet. Milk does not give puppies worms, nor does it cause worms in older dogs. Raw meat does not give them worms. Worm eggs may be present in the ground, in the food, if dirty, or in the bedding. But clean milk and clean meat do not cause them.

Vegetables are not poison. True, in the Stone Age, dogs were carnivorous; so were men. But we no longer live on raw meat knocked off with bows and arrows in the hunt, so why should dogs be limited to a prehistoric diet? The anti-carrot school has a full membership, and so has the anti-tomato.

The truth is that as the world pattern of life has changed for mankind, the pattern has changed for dogdom. Vitamins have moved in.

Meat should be the basic food, or at any rate, protein, and lean chopped beef or horsemeat is tops. Milk, eggs, non-starchy vegetables added to it, with some dry cereal such as shredded wheat, pablum, or cornflakes, make a good general diet. We have tried out various diets for years, and have finally settled on one that gives excellent results.

Puppies from ten weeks to six months should have four meals a day. *Breakfast:* warm milk with dry cereal, melba toast, or puppy biscuit in it. A beaten raw egg, or a teaspoonful of Karo syrup may alternate with the cereal. As a special treat an egg or two scrambled with a little milk in it is warmly received.

Noon and night: chopped beef or horsemeat, raw or cooked, cooked lamb, chicken, or fish. Mix with a little broth or milk, and begin adding vegetables. A teaspoonful is enough at first, but gradually increase the amount until vegetables make up about one-fifth of the meal. Tomatoes, celery, lettuce, green or wax beans, spinach, are all good.

We use carrots for older dogs, but not for puppies.

Starchy vegetables are taboo according to the experts. A dog's stomach does not digest starch as readily as ours do. Potatoes should be omitted, though some dogs seem to thrive on potatoes and gravy, and navy and lima beans and cooked cereals are in the same class. Rice now and then, and barley, we find are readily digested when added to soups or stews.

Bedtime snack: same as breakfast.

From six to ten months of age, three meals a day are sufficient, and subsequently most dogs are happy with two. A mature dog may manage on one meal a day, but we believe that a good morning meal and a light supper are better than to force the dog to get his entire quota in one large feeding.

Before the war we used to buy canned mackerel or the cheaper grades of salmon by the case, and substitute it for meat twice a week. Now we use a canned fish that is put up for cats, and the dogs seem to enjoy that almost as much. Canned dog food is helpful in managing the diet, but the cheaper grades contain so much filler that they are deficient in calories, and probably also in vitamins and minerals.

When the O. P. A. decided to ignore the canine population, owners of single dogs were able to give up their red points and dine on macaroni while Topper ate the meat. Some kennels were closed down, and many owners of dogs went through a distracting period trying to establish a satisfactory substitute diet. Two things saved the day. The first was the vastly increased availability of inspected horsemeat, which has proved to be excellent, fed either raw or canned. The second was the improved quality of many of the commercial dried meals and kibbles which are manufactured for dogs. The best of these provide a scientifically balanced diet for grown dogs and older puppies if meat and fat are added.

And the meat may be hearts, kidneys, livers, or even lungs of beef, pork, or lamb. These should always be cooked well, however. Your dog will assure you that they make an agreeable change.

The proportions of the ingredients which we use are four pounds of dog meal, one pound of meat, and four to six ounces of fat. If you have no clean, fresh drippings to use, buy some good suet, and either dice it or try it out before adding it.

When the puppy is two months old he may be changed over to dog meal by adding a small amount to his milk, and gradually increasing it until the meal has been dampened only enough to make it crumbly.

Now as to method. A very young puppy should be weaned on the beaten yolk of an egg added to milk. We have the best results with evaporated milk. Bottled or raw milk may vary, but the canned milk is always the same. As the puppy's stomach is very small, we use the undiluted evaporated milk at first so that his food is as concentrated as possible. After a time the milk is diluted gradually until he is getting half water and half milk.

The first solid food may be pablum stirred into the egg and milk until it is just slightly thickened. Scraped raw beef in a patty about the size of your thumbnail may be fed about the time the mother is losing interest in running a dairy.

By eight weeks the puppy has a stomach that will adjust to good solid meals. They should always be fed at room temperature, and the food should be chopped up in small pieces. In fact we lay the rugged health of our cockers largely to the fact that we follow these two rules.

There is a wide divergence in present day thought about bones for dogs. Some veterinarians insist that bones only wear down the dog's teeth, while others feel that chewing bones will keep the dog's teeth clean. However, most puppies, and older dogs too, love bones, not only to chew but to play with, and provided you use sense in the bones they are allowed to have, no real damage ever seems to be done. And nothing distracts Towser from your best slippers like a good meaty bone.

The very best bone is cracked knuckle bone, preferably veal or lamb. We feel that this soft bone, filled with calcium and other minerals, is an actual supplement to the diet. Shin bones sawed in short lengths so the marrow can be gotten out are also first class. But never give a dog any bone which you can break in your hands, or which will splinter. Small sharp bones, or chicken bones may make a rush trip to the hospital necessary.

Hard dog biscuits should be given frequently. They are nutritious, and give the dog the chance to chew and crunch which he enjoys.

For extra reinforcement in the diet, a teaspoonful of cod-liver oil each day may be given by spoon, or added to the food. This is a must in winter, but it is an open question whether it is needed in summer unless your dog gets little opportunity to be in the full sun. Too much cod-liver oil, like any other fat, acts almost like mineral oil, and may give the dog diarrhea. Dogs differ in their ability to assimilate fats.

If your dog is getting a balanced diet, he will not need any of the supplementary vitamins and minerals so glowingly advertised. However, if he is high-strung or nervous, ten drops of wheat germ oil in each meal may make him less tense. And it does wonders for his coat!

Our growing puppies get one-half teaspoonful of finely ground bone meal added to their breakfast every day, and about an ounce of tomato juice. Calcium is also a must for matrons in whelp or nursing their puppies. We use calcium gluconate or calcium lactate, crush two five-grain tablets, and add it to their food three times a day. There is no question that this helps prevent eclampsia.

And when you take your own vitamins to give

you that radiant health and bounding vitality and lustrous hair and sparkling eyes that the ads promise, you had better pop one in Rover's open mouth, too. He will roll it with a thoughtful tongue, spit it out, and wait while you crawl under the sofa to get it. When you are prone he will pounce on you and you will both have a wonderful time.

The amount of food for a meal depends upon the age and size of the dog. A teacupful at a meal is about right for an eight-weeks-old puppy. Find out from your own pet about the servings. If he acts ravenous and tries to eat the glaze off the bowl, you are skimping him. If he rolls a dreamy eye, stops to play a game, and then says politely, "Oh, well, may as well please you," and slowly returns to his food, he has too much to eat. Don't leave uneaten food in his bowl after he has had time to wrap himself around it. Take it up.

Always put the bowl in the same place and preferably let him eat quietly. Any dog will refuse to eat if he is over-excited, or if people keep moving around him and his bowl.

Most families have some table scraps even in times like these, and they are excellent if they are not entirely potatoes. Leftover creamed vegetables are fine, and the remains of a soft custard or a soufflé will be thankfully put away. Whenever you have a fowl, or a roast with bones, a fine soup can be made by simmering the bones and scraps, yes, and some fat, to make a good, rich broth. We pop these in a kettle, add a little salt, and cover with cold water. When this simmers nicely we add onion, garlic, lettuce, spinach, tomatoes, chard, cabbage, beet tops—whatever is around all finely chopped. Barley may be added, or rice, shredded wheat, or dog biscuits, dry bread or dog meal, to thicken it.

Invariably when such a soup is simmering, the members of the family will drift by, and stop and sniff and say wistfully, "I suppose we can't have any of that? It's all for the dogs?"

So much for the rules. Maybe your dog will fall in with them happily, or perhaps you may always be saying, "Now, darling, do eat your spinach." In a litter of five puppies, you are apt to have five different feeding problems. We have had several puppies who were allergic to drinking milk. Now and then a dog will have a life-long dislike of fish. We had one puppy who loved tomato juice and would drink it from a cup, and another who wouldn't eat a meal that had even a teaspoonful of tomato juice hidden in it.

If your dog has a certain vegetable he doesn't care for, he will usually go over his bowl and pick out the bits of that one vegetable and lay them aside. He won't eat his carrots just to prevent night-blindness nor his beet tops to get the iron.

If he develops a passion for one kind of food, he will let you know that, too. One of our best boys had such a love of fresh bread that rules, or no rules, he used to have a slice whenever he came to the kitchen and stood up on his hind legs and made suggestive noises.

He was a beautiful big parti-color, strong and vigorous, and if the bread damaged him, it never showed upon his health chart. He didn't care for cake, but bread was his passion.

Then Sister came along, just to really put us in our places in this feeding business. Sister wouldn't touch a bone, she would walk around it. As for raw chopped beef, we could take it right back and cook it decently, said Sister, so a girl could enjoy it. She would starve rather than eat raw meat.

Star was mad about caviar, popcorn, and chocolate. Roquefort cheese was also her dish. We never knew how she got that way, but she made it perfectly clear to us.

Candy and rich cake and cookies are definitely not on the list, but an occasional nibble with the family is not going to put your dog in the stomach ulcer ward. Fried foods are not recommended.

A healthy dog likes to eat. When he loses his appetite something is wrong. Get out the thermometer and take his temperature, but don't try to force food down him if he rejects it. At the first symptoms of failing appetite, try changing his diet and see if he eats better. If not, watch for illness of some sort.

But remember how quick a puppy is to realize

that he has a stranglehold on your heart. I know one sophisticated little black cocker who only eats when her plate is properly placed at the feet of her mistress at the dinner table. If the family eat out, someone has to sit at the table just the same, while she eats.

I knew a dog once who would only eat if her food were tossed in the air so she could catch it, and make a game of it. And I once heard a distracted owner confess that she got down on the floor and pretended to eat out of the puppy's bowl, just to be a good influence.

Now all this, I say openly, is nonsense. I don't blame the dog either! The best way to avoid such carrying-on is never to start it. Nearly any puppy when first removed from the competitive atmosphere of the kennel will sit back and eye his new food languidly. There's nobody to fight for it, so why bother? This is not the time to begin tricks. Let the puppy feel that feeding himself is his own concern. Give him plenty of exercise and plenty of fresh water, and put his meals down regularly in the same place in the same bowl. If you want to peek around the door, do it unobtrusively.

If he won't eat after this treatment, take him to the veterinarian and the high colonic irrigation will undoubtedly clear his system of the buttons, rug lint, fur tippet, rubber bands and hairpins that have already filled his hopeful insides to no avail.

STILLMEADOW SEDUCTIVE (Three months old)

RONNIE HAS PERFECT EARS AND HEAD

☆ ☆ ☆ ☆ ☆ 10 ☆ ☆ ☆ ☆ ☆

How much training you give your dog depends on what your idea of fun really is. Now an untrained dog can do a lot of amusing things, such as pulling out light cords and short-circuiting the whole house, or removing the books from the lower shelves of the bookcases and scalloping the edges. Spaniels have a lot of imagination, and I don't care what the psychologists say about animals not thinking, I say that dogs either think or use some more superior process half the time.

A trained dog, on the other hand, may not be as funny, but he will be a better companion to you. A dog that bites the elevator man is not as easy to go places with as a dog that sits quietly, facing the front, and waits for his floor.

On city streets, a dog that floats along on a leash is a different proposition from a dog that pulls and drags you along, gets in everybody's way and keeps you weaving madly through the crowd. It is possible to track back and forth often enough to get to your destination, but just try carrying an armload of packages with one of those uninhibited dogs at the business end of the leash.

I may as well say flatly, risking the hatred of many dog-lovers, that a dog who pulls his owner all over the street is a nuisance. He has bad manners and they reflect on you more than on him. Not that a certain amount of quartering the field and squirrel chasing isn't inevitable when you take a walk, but that when you say firmly, "Heel," your dog should fall in politely and walk along without yanking your arms from their sockets.

I speak feelingly on this subject because we have had both types of cockers. The dogs we never bothered to train in their youth, are just as apt to rush out in the middle of traffic as to stay on the sidewalk. I have often been dragged out with one of these, while the buses made wide circles around us and cab drivers swore loudly. Or the dog will wind himself around passing pedestrians with most unfortunate results.

He will gee and haw at crossings until you miss the green light, and he will leap happily in the first automobile that has an open door and fold his hands and wait to be taken for a ride.

This not only is hard work for you, but it actually does little to make non-doggy people feel that dogs should be allowed in civilian life. In the city, your dog can make a wonderful impression if he behaves well, or he can do his bit toward laws that bar him from elevators, keep him out of certain restaurants and generally discriminate against him.

Even a dog that never goes to the city should

know enough to walk at heel quietly when he is asked to. He is not so apt to get involved with neighbor's chickens or other dogs or to go off after a hapless cow.

Correctly training a puppy requires patience and good temper on the part of the owner. It ought not to be necessary to say that a dog should not be whipped for failing to understand, but not so long ago I heard a professional man of supposed intelligence say he was the only one in the family that could "handle" the cocker. "I throw the telephone book at him," he said happily. Then he complained because the dog was timid!

If you call your puppy to you and then whack him, you may scare him into fits, but you won't train him. Probably once in a dog's life, he may need a spanking. But after you go to him and take a folded newspaper to his hindquarters, you will find out it is the tone of your voice that really cuts him to the quick. Especially spaniels! They respond immediately to the tone of voice, registering joy, excitement, sorrow, shame, according to the sound. A word of praise raises them to a pitch of happiness, and a sharp scolding casts them to utter depths.

The best way to train your puppy is to form a happy association with what you want him to do. A bit of cookie, warm praise, a kiss or two on the soft muzzle, these are infallible aids in training.

Eight weeks is old enough to begin kindergarten. The puppy should be in a place where there are no distractions, and the first lesson should be to sit at command, or "hup". Some authorities begin with heeling, but I am in favor of sitting first. It is a basic bit of training, and it is easy.

With a tidbit in one hand, get the puppy's attention and give the command, in a serious tone of voice. Repeat it several times, and push the hindquarters gently to the floor. When the puppy sits down, usually with an expression of great surprise on his face, present him with the reward and tell him how superior he is. Get another tidbit and try again. Never work more than twenty minutes with young puppies—like children they are easily distracted and their attention wanders. After twenty minutes they want to make spitballs or pull somebody's pigtail.

When the puppy sits nicely for the tidbit, omit it, and instead, raise your hand, with first finger up in a cautioning way. This almost duplicates the way you held your hand with the bit of cookie in it, and he should recognize the gesture. When he is clear that this means the same thing, gradually increase the length of time he sits in position; then slowly back away a step or two, saying "Stay!". Eventually you will be able to have him sit for several minutes, out of your way, while you get the roast in the oven. If you accompany your command by gesturing with the flat of your hand toward his little black nose, it will not be long before this signal can replace your spoken command. Don't forget to praise him lavishly whenever he does what you ask him to do, and after you are sure he knows what you want, scold him a little if he does not immediately do as you order. The words "No!" or "Naughty" spoken in a tone of disapproval, are usually enough punishment for a Spaniel.

And, by the way, from the very first he should be learning what NO means. Try to be consistent about using the word. Don't say, "No!" one time, and, "Stop that!" the next. And above all else, never say no or give him any other command when you haven't the time to see that he carries it out. If you can't drop whatever else you are doing and see that your order is successfully carried out, just skip the whole thing for the time being.

Now about this business of walking properly beside you when you take that afternoon saunter through the park or do the errands. This is called heeling and every puppy should be taught to heel, whether he lives in the city or on a farm. Even in the country the day may come when he must go to town with you, or accompany you on a trip, and you and he will both be regarded as better citizens if you can accomplish the matter with some dignity and style.

The first step is to get the baby a light collar that fits him. Put this on him and let him play around with it on for a day or two. When he is so used to it that he has forgotten it, pick him up in your arms and carry him a hundred yards or so from the house. Snap on the leash, and set him down beside you. Normally he will head for the house, which he knows; so follow along, keeping the leash as loose as possible so he will feel no restraint. Let him lead you wherever he wishes to go, and try to make it fun. Talk to him in a pleasant, encouraging tone. When he gets back to the house with you, carry him back down the road, a little farther this time.

When he has gotten the idea that this new game is just fine, it is time to let him take you for walks in other directions. Now you begin to use the leash to control him. But do it gently, and not by dragging him around, but by giving the leash small, intermittent twitches. From the first you have tried to keep him on your left, where he will be trained to walk, shoulder even with your left ankle. Try to bring him into this position as often as possible, but don't be too insistent with a young puppy.

If you persist, the day will come when he is more often in the correct position than not. From that point on use the command "Heel!" and keep him at your left ankle by a twitch of the leash whenever he starts to wander. If he is naturally a sledge dog, who wants to drag you after him, your measures will have to be somewhat firmer. Whenever he gets ahead of you, turn sharply and reverse your steps. *After* you have turned, give a quick jerk on the leash. Since your back is turned to him when you do this, he will usually blame himself for the jerk, and will begin to watch you more closely, and follow you with more care.

The next step should be simple, for you will combine two things which he already knows, heel and sit. Command him to heel, and after walking for a few seconds, stop. Tell him to sit. He should sit straight beside you, facing the way you are. Start ahead once more, giving him the command, "Heel". Halt again and tell him to sit. Forward again, halt again, each time with the command he knows. It will not be long before you can drop the command to sit, for he will be doing it automatically each time you stop.

When he heels nicely at one pace, vary it. Walk slowly, or run a few paces. Turn sharply right or left until he follows your steps perfectly. And keep the leash loose. Tighten it quickly for a second only to correct him, or to warn him of what you expect of him if the neighbor's cat runs enticingly across the road.

When he is letter perfect, you may remove the leash, if you are where you will not be arrested. Proceed exactly as before, giving your commands confidently. You will have the thrill of knowing that Prince no longer needs a leash, except as a concession to law and order. He is ready for lunch at the Ritz.

There is one more thing that is an essential of

every dog's education. He should come when he is called. Most dogs do this so naturally that few of us ever consider that it should become an ingrained habit of obedience, both for our own convenience and for the dog's safety and welfare. As soon as the puppy knows his name, begin by kneeling down to his level, and calling persuasively, "Prince, come!". Even a tiny puppy will usually respond by wobbling to you. If he hesitates at all, pat your knee, and give the command again, in a warm tone. Reward him by a great deal of praise, move away, and try it again. Little by little increase the distance from which you call him, and never fail to give him a tidbit or real praise when he comes.

As he gets older, and you expect him to come even though it means leaving a game, or the scent of a rabbit, or a beautiful bone, always greet him with a word of praise and affection. From his point of view, he has made a sacrifice to obey you, and done it cheerfully.

Retrieving is a good habit, even if you never plan to send him after pheasant. It is grand exercise for your dog in a limited space, and is fun for both of you. Most baby Spaniels retrieve with enthusiasm. At first use only one object, a ball, if you like, or a clean rag tied in a knot. Keep this one object just for retrieving, and soon the little fellow will know when he sees it that you are going to have a game.

At first throw the ball a short distance and say "fetch" or "get it", and if he brings it back, praise him. He is more apt to bring it back to the starting point if you choose one of his favorite spots—the best sofa or the chair he sleeps in. He already has a pattern of return to that place.

If he refuses to bring it back, put his leash on, and gently bring him back to you. Reward him, and repeat the process until he gets the idea and comes galloping to you, tail beating and face wreathed in smiles.

My first dog was a born retriever. He once retrieved a lovely fresh rolled roast of beef from somebody's back door and brought it home without even breaking the paper. He was a Setter who wanted to do his bit for the family.

And once I had what we called a Water Spaniel whose specialty was bringing home the bacon in the form of dead fish. We were spending the summer on a fresh water lake, and all the fish in the lake must have had Chinese rot that season. There were literally hundreds of dead fish that Brownie was able to bring in. I was reading Shakespeare, Keats, and Shelley that summer, and nothing was more of a shock than to raise my eyes from *"some shape of beauty that moves away the pall from our dark spirits"*, to see Brownie loping up with a desiccated offering of whitefish.

My father said I had to bury whatever Brownie

brought home. Consequently I kept the shovel right beside the hammock.

A natural retriever will now and then come in with a live chicken. In that case, you probably will have to pay the neighbors for a whole flock. There is very little to say about this situation. It simply exists. A bout with a porcupine is even worse, and goes under ailments, farther on in this discussion.

To see an Obedience Trial is to become a fanatic at once. The sight of a dozen assorted dogs heeling, slowing, doubling, retrieving, jumping over hurdles to bring back their dumbells, sitting without a sign of anguish while their owners go away—this is a sight for dog lovers to write home about.

At the first Obedience Trial I witnessed, a Beagle, a Welsh Corgi, a Shetland Sheep Dog, a Sealyham, a Boxer, and a Spaniel were in the ring. They went through such intricate tests as retrieving their master's glove, picking their master's possession out of a welter of scattered things, stopping in the midst of a recall, marching left and right and slow and double. There was a broad jump, too, and when the little Corgi came to it he went up and looked it over, laid one paw on the barrier, and shook his head, and went back to his owner. He was right, too, he never could have spanned it.

"A word of praise is allowed between exercises," says the manual. The word of praise usually consisted of the master catching the dog up in his arms and indulging in a love feast. I enjoyed seeing the massive Boxer kissed rapturously by his master. This Boxer had some trouble with scent; he proudly retrieved a shoehorn from the pile, instead of his master's wallet.

One of the most touching sights I know is a line of dogs in an Obedience ring sitting motionless and mute while their handlers walk away from them. Not a muscle twitches down the line, but the eyes follow the departing backs of the owners with such yearning and longing and such love and loyalty that I usually weep behind my catalogue.

The important thing about these tests is that they are not tricks. They are practical. And when a dog has finally received an official Obedience Degree, he will be able to conduct himself in almost any crisis thereafter.

Most dogs are eager to learn. They are not lazy, and they like to have jobs to do. A friend of mine was training a young bitch in Obedience Work. An older dog was in the house at the time, watching from a nearby sofa. Before long the older dog dropped down and fell in behind the youngster, and copied her behavior, dropping when she dropped, trotting when she trotted, heeling gracefully after her mistress.

Training for hunting or for field trials is more specialized a subject than may be taken up here.

If you hunt, you may train your Spaniel to be a perfect gun-dog, or send him to one of the professional trainers who will do the job for you. The same applies to getting your dog ready for field trials. Over a period of centuries, the cocker has established himself as a hunter second to none.

If you only go out to knock off a few crows, your Spaniel will be delighted to go along and bring the game in.

☆ ☆ ☆ ☆ ☆ 11 ☆ ☆ ☆ ☆ ☆

This section is devoted particularly to those individuals who feel that if one thing is good, more is better. In other words, wouldn't it be fine to have a family of little round soft puppies just like Mamma? Or how about a son and heir for that gay boy?

There may possibly be other things in this world that are more satisfying than a new litter of puppies, but if so, I have never found them. Four or five button-nosed wiggling fat babies rolling around, staggering on wobbly legs toward the milk dish, sitting down suddenly on fat little behinds, once you know the enchantment of actually owning such, you are to all intents and purposes a breeder, even if you have only a three-room city apartment and one brood matron.

Raising puppies is not a lazy man's job, however. It involves more on your part than a kiss now and then on a velvet-soft muzzle. Yes, indeed, it does. You have to like practical nursing for the very young. You have to be willing to sit up half the night if necessary, and miss a few social engagements. By and large, you do quite a lot of work. And then one day, after the babies have their eyes open, you go up to the pen and the entire gang comes rushing over, wagging with joy. "Ah, here you are!" they say, "how wonderful!" Well, it's worth it.

If you are breeding a dog, you should always seek to produce puppies that are a little bit better than the parents. If you don't know about linebreeding, at least choose a stud that seems to correct any obvious faults in the bitch. For a small weedy bitch, for example, find a stud with plenty of bone and a good body. If your pet has ears on top of her head, try not to marry her off to the first dog that rolls along whose ears are also as high as a radio aerial. It is true that the puppies will inherit also characteristics of grandparents and forefathers but still the parents themselves are very influential. We have a red stud that persistently sires puppies with the same naïve eyes, set wide and large. Another, a bitch, has a slightly slanting eye placement, which is bad as far as show points are concerned, but most charming to see. So far as we know, her famous champion ancestors had eyes just like other champions. But Sister will take her favorite child out for the Easter Parade and both look about with the same slanting smile.

Planning your puppies makes breeding one of the most fascinating jobs in the world. Breeding out certain traits of shyness, or nervousness, breeding in physical characteristics that are outstanding, breeding for beauty and personality, making mistakes, and trying again—this is a constantly challenging field and one whose interest never stales.

The service of a good stud dog costs from twenty-five to fifty dollars usually, with higher prices for the larger breeds. It is not always a good thing, however, to take your lady under your arm and dash off to the nearest champion. Champions do not always beget champions. Sometimes also a champion will be used so much that his actual vitality may be lessened.

A stud dog needs a good sound ancestry behind him, and the tendency to sire puppies that are true to type. The ability to transmit quality is often possessed by a dog that is not himself a bench show champion. The famous Red Brucie never became a champion. Some dogs seem to be born studs, and some are not. The only positive indication of the dog's ability is to see some puppies he has already sired in previous litters.

The first question prospective breeders ask is, "Now, what color will the puppies be?"

Spaniels have the most varied assortment of allowable color combinations of any breed, which is one reason for having them. You can always gamble with yourself on what the new Fall colors will be. Color breeding is too technical to dismiss over a canapé or a teacup but there are laws by which you can breed and get exactly the color you desire.

In general these breeding laws are no more intelligible to a lay mind than the color variations in humans. But it is necessary to understand that certain colors are dominant in some cockers, and others are recessive. The color of the litter depends on what colors are dominant in the sire and dam, and which are recessive and how the dominants and recessives combine. Simple, isn't it?

For instance, you are wild about solid blacks and you bought yourself a neat little solid black girl, and you breed her happily to a black sire. And what do you get? Well, maybe the solid black girl had a parti-color mamma and the black sire came from a dark red father. In other words, neither of the blacks may be pure blacks. And when the blessed event occurs, you may be considerably amazed at the light red puppies, the red and whites, and the solitary little black and white.

Our first litter was obtained by breeding a solid black bitch to a parti-color sire. The black bitch had a black and white mother, and a black father and a grandfather who was fire red. The sire came from a line of red and whites and black and whites.

We had six little darlings born on the sofa. They were all different. A dark red and white, a liver and white, a light red and white, a black and white, a buff, and a dark red. What we wanted was solid blacks.

Now, we learned after a while that a pure black is dominant over all other colors. That means a dog of black parents, not a red dog that happens to have a black coat. A pure black will produce black puppies no matter if he or she is mated to a patchwork quilt. Most black cockers are hybrids in color ancestry, and are not pure blacks.

Dark mahogany red is difficult to get. The red shades vary from cream to a kind of light oak varnish color. The reds are either brown nosed or black nosed. These have dark eyes, dark footpads, dark edged eyelids, dark spots on the gums for the black nosed, and brown for the brown nosed.

Two brown nosed reds will usually produce red puppies. The black nosed red sire is likely to throw reds. But an almost certain way of obtaining Irish setter reds is to breed a dark nosed red to solid black, dark nosed red again to solid black, or to a black who has a red parent.

We used a red stud with black nose. Bred to a black and white parti-color with about seven generations of black and whites behind her, we got five puppies, four light reds and one solid black! The same sire bred to a solid color silver buff resulted in five silver buffs.

After all, there's no use getting a headache over the probable color of the puppies. After you see them, any color goes. The dog under the coat is what matters. I began by thinking only solid black was perfect. Then we got a black and white.

I made a stand then against light buffs. Anything but buff, I said. So now a shining moon-color dog is my favorite of all colors. Unless you consider deep fire red. And then that reddish orange is pretty nice, too.

The reds and red and whites tend to have ears not as well furred, often rather stringy. Their coats are not as deep as the blacks. A smooth body coat is the most desirable in any color, with the ears wavy.

When you have chosen the stud, the next little item is the actual breeding. A single breeding is sufficient. Wearing both dogs out by repeated breeding does them no good and does not insure puppies.

The time to breed differs with different bitches. Some will stand for the stud much earlier in the heat than others. Generally the best time, is just past the middle of the heat. No hard and fast date can be set, from the tenth to fourteenth day is usually all right. In the early part of the period the bitch will not have any traffic with the male, then as the flow diminishes comes the time when her stars are in the right aspect. As the bitch grows older, the season shortens and breeding should come earlier.

A bitch should not be bred at her first season. She may be full grown, but she actually is not mature enough to undertake the hazards of childbearing, not to mention raising the tender little things. And, further, no matter how much enthusiasm you have, you should not breed her more than once a year. A period of rest is indicated after she has sent the puppies away to college. She should have time to go to a few concerts and lectures or take up athletics before she again begins the duties in the nursery.

Mismating is an unfortunate occurrence, but it does not affect the subsequent litters. Dozens and dozens of frantic people have written me saying, "What shall we do? Bonnie has had a litter by mistake and now we can never have any thoroughbreds again." Every breeding is a separate matter, a law unto itself.

It is hard to be patient with people who leave the back door open while assorted kinds of setters, terriers, collies and wind-hounds assemble around the porch. For once a breeding has taken place, you have to take it and like it. The puppies ought not to be saved, except as pets, but what a hard heart it takes to give away the newborn helpless innocents!

Discretion is decidedly the better part of valour. You should keep the bitch safely away from temptation until you are ready to approve of the whole affair. There are a number of preparations to be had which discourage male pursuit. I have mentioned the citronella and lemon spray. But you cannot depend on this or any preparation to prevent a breeding, if the time is right for it.

You may encourage yourself to hope for the best if your bitch has been at large, by giving a douche of half-vinegar and half-water as soon as you can gather your erring one in. The sooner the better. It at least gives you something to do. There is a new hormone preparation, which if injected promptly by a veterinarian, may keep the bitch from conceiving even though she has been bred.

A good stud is worth whatever you pay for his services. You buy the result of years of breeding, you give your coming puppies a guarantee that they will be standard in quality. All dogs are not created free and equal by any means, and superior blood produces better stock.

You are entitled to one return service if the first breeding has missed. At no extra expense, let me add. Sometimes a female will miss the first time, even though she may afterward be a great-great-grandmother many times over. But often people who have had a female for eight or ten years suddenly become seized with a fever to have some puppies before she goes to the undiscovered bourne from which no spaniel returns.

Probably there won't be any puppies if the happy idea came too late in life. A bitch who has regular litters will go on producing puppies over a good long period but an unbred female gets over the notion after a while.

A proven stud, that is, a male who has sired litters, and a proven brood matron, that is, one who has brought up families, will be pretty certain to produce litters. A young untried male may not beget puppies at first. Wheat germ is the favorite aid to correct sterility. This comes in many forms, and most drug stores carry some preparation based on wheat germ.

☆ ☆ ☆ ☆ ☆ 12 ☆ ☆ ☆ ☆ ☆

The puppies will be born from the fifty-ninth to the sixty-third day after breeding. This gives you plenty of leeway, days in which to tear your hair and pace the floor and stay awake at night listening. If you are nervous and high-strung, you will be sure they are coming the fifty-ninth day and then you will worry yourself sick the rest of the time. If, on the other hand, you are on the stolid side you won't lift an eyebrow until the sixty-third day, and if they come earlier you simply won't be ready.

Three weeks after she is bred, the female must be wormed. This is the deadline. If you forget it then, you will have to omit worming and have your troubles later with the puppies.

For eight weeks the bitch can have her normal diet and exercise. Toward the end of the period she will begin to eat less. The diet should be slightly laxative as she has to eliminate extra waste products. A pinch of soda in the drinking water is advisable during the last week, and three days before you expect the puppies, give a teaspoonful of milk of magnesia once a day.

Many breeders omit all vegetables for the last week or two weeks. But I keep to the regular diet, especially since plain meat is a little constipating. Eggs and milk are good for calcium, and calcium may also be given in crushed tablets added to the food, or in a powder form sold at drug stores under various trade names. Cod-liver oil or haliver oil capsules should be given. As the time for the puppies' birth approaches, smaller meals are better for the bitch, and more frequent feeding. A soda cracker or a bit of buttered toast given for "morning sickness" is a help.

As the time for the puppies nears, you will fix a whelping box, line it with torn clean newspapers and assemble the simple equipment. The box must be large enough so that the bitch won't have to sit down flat on her progeny when she gets in with them. Most factory-built boxes for whelping have a little shelf around three sides, the theory being that when Mamma sits on the babies, they will at least be able to squirm under the shelf and get a chance to breathe. Warmth you must have, and cleanliness and quiet.

Notwithstanding these requirements, I know a breeder who has the puppies in an unheated shed in the dead of winter and takes pride in the fact that they can stand it. Of course some human babies are born in railroad stations and taxis, too, but I shouldn't call it ideal.

After you get the whelping box all fixed, and if

your home carpenter has built it, after you have wrapped up his bruised thumb and put iodine on the nail scratches, you show the new contraption proudly to the expectant mother. Chances are she gives it a smell or two and goes away, nose in air. She herself then selects her own spot, either under the briars in the rose bed, or on the handmade heirloom quilt on the best bed. (One of the loveliest surprises of my childhood was when my father was looking for a clean shirt one morning, and opened his bureau drawer and there were six kittens in it.)

In the years we have been raising spaniels we have had several very correct whelping rooms set aside in the kennels, tried out various boxes, set up cots in special rooms so that we could doze off a minute during the night. But the puppies practically always arrive in my bedroom. Any sick dog on the place flies at once to the same room; they feel better there. No matter how many times we set up a whelping place, when the hour arrives, the mother seeks sanctuary in the bedroom, and that is that. We then make the room over temporarily into a hospital ward and everything is fine.

Now and then we have gotten things started in another place and had the mother move the puppies already born to my sofa while we were out in the kitchen filling the hot-water bottle.

This is what we keep in the whelping kit: A

spool of very strong white thread. A bottle of olive oil. Iodine. Cotton. Scissors, sterilized. Gauze. We never use the gauze, but it seems more scientific to have it.

Aside from this, you need a small box lined with old flannel pajamas, or soft cloths and two hot-water bottles—one will do but two saves frequent trips to the kitchen. A pile of soft clean towels or a box of the new disposable baby diapers is handy.

All this sounds very silly to people who believe a dog should have puppies under the barn and if half of them die at birth—well there are still enough left. But if you have a good dog and go to the bother of breeding, you want to save the puppies entire, and be sure the mother is all right. A little extra care makes the difference.

☆ ☆ ☆ ☆ ☆ 13 ☆ ☆ ☆ ☆ ☆

About the fifty-eighth day, you can throw away your calendar, and use your intelligence to tell you about when the puppies will be born. I have known people who lost the whole litter and then the bitch, too, because they went to a dinner party and the bitch had the family while they were gone.

These people simply weren't intelligent. The fact is, nature gives you plenty of hints. A couple of days before the puppies are coming, the shape of the bitch changes. The litter begins to settle down and the mother actually looks thinner to a casual eye. The hip bones stand out, and in spaniels especially, the skin of the bitch has a loose appearance instead of being tight as a drum. The weight shifts down lower in the body and the nipples swell.

Then, after wolfing her food for weeks, there comes a meal which the mother looks at and from which she turns away. If she refuses her supper, phone your friends that you may not make a fourth at bridge the next night. Some dogs eat right up to the end, but after eating the last big meal, throw it up intact in a little while. Nature is getting ready for business.

This indication is something nobody ever told me about, but it is my primary notice that the crisis is at hand. I always watch the last few days to see how the dog is eating.

The next period is the nest-building time. This isn't as sure as the meal test because some maternal spaniels begin to make nests days and days before they need to. But insistent scratching up of upholstery or whipping around of sofa cushions or shredding of papers means something. When you let the bitch out for a run, watch how she behaves. If she jumps down in the opening to the cellar windows, or begins to uproot the peony bed, or crawls under the barn or garage floor, you may know that you may expect puppies soon.

Labor itself begins with panting, shaking, quivering and a curious withdrawn expression in the eyes. The tongue hangs out and the panting gradually becomes more rapid. This goes on, with intervals of rest, for some time. Usually it is at least two hours and it may be ten before the first puppy is born.

If the period is prolonged beyond reason, a veterinarian must be consulted, but never try to hurry labor by forced means, such as castor oil. Nature really knows best. There are breeds of dogs that have too much difficulty whelping and need Caesareans, but if you have such a bitch, you have been forewarned before you bred her at all.

In due time, the first puppy will be born, coming into the world neatly wrapped in his own cellophane sac, a little rolled-up ball of infinite potentialities. If the puppy comes head first, sac intact, you may stand by and simply wipe the sweat from your own brow.

If, however, the sac is broken and the puppy has a dry birth, you may be needed. There is danger at this point of the puppy being strangled or not properly delivered. You may grasp the puppy gently with a sterile piece of gauze wrapped around your hand and very gently turn and draw the little body outward.

If the puppy is born hind end first, there is more need for your assistance lest he suffocate. Every puppy has his own after-birth and these must all be accounted for, as a retained after-birth will cause tragedy for the matron later.

Most matrons will break the cellophane sac themselves and get the puppy breathing, cut the umbilical cord and push the baby around until it begins to nurse, clean up the after-birth and continue to wash and polish the newborn infant until the next baby arrives. But now and then a sensitive high-strung mother will simply stare with a shocked and horrified look at this wriggling bundle. If so, you must immediately break the sac over the puppy's nose and open his mouth with your little finger and be sure breathing is established.

That first thin wail of a newborn puppy as he draws outer air in his lungs is miracle enough for anybody. The next minute, you will see him begin to pull toward his mother, and I have seen puppies even begin to nurse before they were completely freed from the sac.

If the mother is not disposed to cut the cord and get the baby cleaned up, you may snip the cord with sterile shears and rub the puppy briskly with a warm soft flannel. The cord should not be cut too close to the body, leave at least half an inch or more. We had one mother who always insisted on managing this task herself and always cut the cords too close, and nearly caused hemorrhages in her offspring.

While the puppies are being born, keep the first ones in a box on hot-water bottles while actual labor is going on, then replace them by the mother as she rests.

The interval between births varies from twenty minutes to several hours. A cocker averages from four to six in a litter, but we had a litter of seven once and after they were all comfortably settled down an eighth one rolled along.

While you are helping out, touch the navels with a drop of iodine to prevent any infection. Then after the puppies are settled down you can stir them up again by giving them each a few drops of warm olive oil in the tip of a teaspoon. The silly little things will scoop their tongues around it and suck loudly, it is a mild laxative and makes sure their insides function easily.

Now the thread is a different proposition. When nature composed the little masterpiece that turns out to be a cocker spaniel, she failed to dock the tails. A spaniel with a long stringy whip at the rear end is an odd sight, and furthermore his habit of violently wagging his way through life can strip an undocked tail to a shred of raw bones. The tail of the cocker should be snipped off, preferably not later than three days after birth. I favor doing it at birth before circulation is set up and the cocker established in the new world. But if the puppies are weak or the mother is having a hard whelping, let well enough alone. Ordinarily the tails may be snipped off and the whole thing forgotten by everybody in a few hours.

The scissors must be dull, preferably surgical shears. Sharp scissors make a sharp cut which bleeds easily. The tail should be clipped fairly short. You can feel with your finger where the cartilage tapers off, this will be roughly a third of the length of the tail. The puppy will not suffer, and even if the cutting is delayed a few days, a single squawk settles the affair as far as he is concerned.

If the tail does not seal itself over but instead begins to ooze, it must be tied off tightly with the thread until a clot can form. Be careful not to leave a long end of thread for the mother to worry off, but trim the knot closely. Never leave this thread on more than overnight. Usually you may remove it in a short time, an hour or so.

If you have not tied the thread tightly enough, the bleeding may continue and in that case you must tighten the knot.

There is always a chance that one or more of the puppies will be born defective. If a puppy seems unable to nurse, you may discover he has a cleft palate. By putting your finger in the mouth and feeling the roof, you will be able to tell whether there is a physical defect there. A harelip will prevent nursing since the puppy will not be able to suck correctly. You must remove these puppies from the litter, for if they remain with the mother and slowly starve to death, she may develop a severe case of nerves and refuse the normal puppies, or she may try to kill the weak ones in her distracted state.

But be sure there is an actual malformation of the mouth, not just that the puppy is too weak to make the effort, or too slow to figure the whole thing out. You may often save puppies by helping them nurse until they are strong enough or have will enough to take care of themselves. This, I may add, takes a lot of patience. Fitting an infinitesimal mouth over the nipple, working the minute jaws, and keeping the bitch still at the same time is quite a trick.

Also the healthy bigger puppies will grab the best meal and leave no place at the table for the weaker ones, so you must repeat your first aid every few hours at first. For supplementary feeding this is the formula: yolk of one egg, 2 tablespoons top milk, 2 tablespoons of water, 1 tablespoon lime water, 1 teaspoon milk sugar.

This should be mixed and kept in a sterile container and fed at body temperature. One dropperful apiece twice a day is sufficient at first provided the mother is nursing the puppies fairly well.

No expert in the world will advise trying to raise a litter from birth without a nursing mother. It is sheer folly to undertake the struggle. But if you are a fiend for punishment and love those helpless little mites beyond all reason, you may not give them over to the dark angel without a struggle.

It takes a grim determination to defeat death, an unflagging zeal, and patience to add to it in order to raise puppies artificially.

At first the puppies need to be fed every hour during the day, about an eighth of an ounce at a time. They will also have to be fed several times during the night. They must be kept warm and dry. The constant rubbing of the mother's warm tongue seems to pour life into them; lacking this, you will have to do the best you can with a soft

TOP HAT LOOKS BACKWARD

THE WORLD IS A VERY LARGE PLACE

warm cloth. Clean the rectum with a little olive oil or vaseline and when the puppies get very dirty, rub off the dirt with a little alcohol on cotton. Feed with a medicine dropper or a baby doll nursing bottle with a small nipple. The amount varies according to the size of the puppies. When the little stomachs are round as golf balls, they have had a square meal.

You can always tell whether a puppy is getting enough food by picking it up. If the puppy feels spudgy and soft like melting soap, and the skin slides around, the puppy is not right. A satisfied puppy feels tonic, even when it falls dead asleep, paws in air and milky mouth closed. You can go over a litter with your eyes shut and identify the weaklings by the feel of them.

The normal mother with a normal litter settles down after the last puppy is born. Then they may be comfortable in the whelping box where they should have been all the time. Clean torn newspapers make the best bedding because cloth is apt to catch on the tiny claws, and the mother has to dig everything up now and then to be sure it is suitable. Papers will not smother the offspring but cloth bedding may. A thick pad of carpet or a crib pad may go under the papers for warmth but it must be flat on the bottom. Safe in the arms of the *Times Book Review*, the babies will acquire a nice cultural background.

Now it is time to drag the reluctant mother

away to stretch for a few moments and relieve herself of accumulated waste products. The overconscientious mother will have to be taken out as often as necessary even if she is sure the goblins will get her babies while she is gone.

For the first day after whelping, the mother should have a very light diet. Milk, broth, or arrowroot pudding. We have found that a nervous mother may refuse everything until a nice bowl of fresh warm arrowroot pudding is set before her. She can't resist this. You can buy the prepared pudding in any grocery store, being sure it has an arrowroot base, not cornstarch.

A bowl of milk and raw eggs set near the water pan for the first few days may tempt her to take more nourishment. Once back on meat, the bitch usually wants to eat an entire roast at a time. Small meals fed frequently is the best rule.

About this time all the neighbors' children from miles around are standing on the doorstep waiting to see the gift of the stork. It is just a question of whether you want to please the visitors or keep your litter. Absolutely no visitors is the rule. One of the saddest stories I know is about a family who had a litter of puppies and entertained admiring company. The desperate mother took the first chance and moved the whole litter under the barn. Since it was winter weather, quite naturally they all died of pneumonia. We lost one of our loveliest litters in the early days of our experience by letting a visitor in to see the cunning mites. The lady brought distemper.

The third reason for isolation is the mother's need for quiet. Eclampsia may be due to calcium deficiency alone, but many a mother "falls over" as the old Scotchman said, because she is overexcited. If she doesn't have eclampsia, her supply of milk may be threatened. Discussion of eclampsia belongs in a later chapter.

Most mothers treat their babies rather roughly. When we had our first litter, I sat up all night wrapped in a comforter reaching down every ten minutes to rescue some squealer from Mamma's digging. Regularly she got up and stirred them round like an egg beater. Actually mothers don't squash their children, once the birth is done with, although frequently puppies are killed accidentally during the whelping if the owner has gone to a dinner party and the frantic mother is having her struggle alone.

However, I still think it advisable to keep within earshot of the new family during the first few hours. This is always during the latter half of the night when you are completely exhausted, but you get so you can sleep heavily and rouse instantly at that tiny scream which means, "Mamma is sitting on me. Help!"

One of the most moving sights I have seen was with golden Honey's first litter. Honey is a big strapping bitch, too bulky for the show ring.

After her puppies were born she stood leaning over the box looking down at them with sheer amazement. She cocked her head on one side, then on the other, her dark eyes filled with wonder. Where in the world, she asked, did these come from? Five miniature golden balls they were, wiggling and rolling around. Then in a moment, she lifted one golden paw and set it gently in the box, with infinite care lifted another paw and set it down in the box and very delicately moved in, nosed her babies in a heap and lowered her big body around them. She was acutely conscious of her weight and their smallness, and when finally she spread her ears over them and looked up, the humans in the room began to swallow lumps in their throats as big as potatoes.

☆ ☆ ☆ ☆ ☆ 14 ☆ ☆ ☆ ☆ ☆

The mother will nurse the growing babies for the first three weeks. Sometimes the puppies may go the full six weeks on their mother's milk. But when the litter is large, early weaning is preferable.

During the nursing period, care must be taken that all the mother's nipples are worked on. Often there are two that the puppies pass by and these may cause caked breasts. It is amazing how stubborn little blind babies can be, paddling fiercely with their wee raspberry paws and screwing up their faces as they declare they absolutely will not be bothered with that particular nipple. You open their mouths and the little pink flannel tongue is already curved like a sugar scoop. They offer to suck your finger, to suck your sleeve, to do almost anything but work on that unused nipple.

But patience wins, they give in finally and do their job to keep the nipples soft.

Caked breasts must be massaged gently with lard and covered with a bandage.

The exact time to begin weaning depends on your guess as to the amount of milk and the health of the mother. From three weeks on, it is better to supplement the mother's milk with outside feeding. For early weaning, use the formula for artificial feeding. For normal weaning, I like best plain undiluted evaporated milk, warm. If we had a Jersey cow, we would use it for the milk bar. But lacking that helpful animal, there is much to be said for milk out of a can. It is uniform in quality, it is easy to use, it is rich and it agrees with the delicate stomachs. As the puppies grow you can dilute the milk with water half and half and have standard milk content.

At the same time that the puppies are wading in the milk pan, they are ready to eat beef scraped with a tablespoon from fresh round steak. Beginning with as much as goes on a thumb nail, by the fifth or sixth week the puppy will be eating all you can take time to scrape. Then you may change over to lean chopped beef.

Few things are as much fun as giving the first meat meal. The puppies are idling in the pen. You set down a saucer with thumb-nail meat tidbits. You pick up a soft baby and hold a meat cake in your palm. There comes the nose, and then all at once light dawns. This, he says, is what he has been waiting for all his life! Oh ecstasy! Oh joy! He makes frantic passes at the meat, breathes it up, chokes, smacks his mouth, swallows, and rushes for more as fast as if he were going to a fire.

A little of the scraped beef in the milk does wonders too.

Prepared baby food may next be added to the milk to make a more solid meal. There are several kinds sold in most drug stores. Arrowroot biscuits crumbled in milk and raw egg are good. Meat broth and puppy meal come next.

Feed the puppies four times a day and keep the mother away for longer and longer intervals. Sometimes when I am fixing a weaning meal, I go out and find three of the puppies are guzzling down their mother's meal, vegetables and all. An infinitesmal mite lugging a slice of roast beef out from under Mamma's nose is pretty cute.

Tomato juice in a teaspoon is a first for the young fry. With every litter I feed it earlier, the same way the mountain people give cabbage water to their nursing infants.

Cod-liver oil may be introduced at about the time solid food is managed easily.

By eight weeks mother can take a trip to Florida and the puppies can tuck their books under their paws and go to school.

Raising a litter may mean a lot of work, and some anxious hours. But as I see four or five stalwart puppies tumbling on the grass, I am always sad that the nursery is empty. No more watching for the first eye to squint open showing soft cloudy blue behind the slit, no more rescuing a fat baby who swims in the milk pan, no more waiting for the first bark, like a doll's house trumpet. Fold up the pen, put away the left-over pads.

Nights are for sleeping now. Nobody falls out of the box and gets lost and cries to deaf heaven. Nobody's nose gets pinched in a door.

Let's hurry and have another litter!

Once we had a litter in a box in the summer kitchen. The little dears were tucked away for the night when somebody heard a rat out there. At the time we were unhappy hosts to rats from the nearby farmer's barn, who liked the summer kitchen especially. Some enterprising ones had gnawed into the dog-food container and I will say there never were such rats as were raised on Blank's dog ration. Super rats!

Somebody sitting by the fire said that rats ate young puppies. In terror we rushed out and moved the box into the living room, upsetting the babies considerably. We then closed up the living room tight, locked the doors and went to bed.

When I got up to open the door in the morning, the first one to rush out to greet me was the rat, who had been shut in all night with the puppies! He was extremely nervous as he dashed away. I no longer believe rats eat puppies, even when they are right at hand, since this experience.

Another old superstition is that mothers kill the babies if they feel like it. A woman once wrote me that her pet dog killed a whole litter by strangling them. I just do not believe it. The puppies in question were dying of pneumonia and I feel sure the mother was trying to lick their throats to aid breathing.

It is true that a mother will push a defective puppy away and if the puppy is left with the rest she may become so nervous that she neglects the whole family. Perhaps in time she might do away with the others, but this I have never seen.

Switching part of a litter to another smaller group may be accomplished by rubbing the newcomers around like animated sponges against the puppies they are to live with. The mother should go for a walk and admire the scenery while the change takes place. When she comes back, she usually looks with surprise at the extra addition to her family, and then practically washes the skin off getting them to smell right. We once put a black and white in a light litter and the adopted mother seemed to like that one better than all the rest, she favored him in every way, almost spoiled him to death. He led the life of Reilly.

Now about bathing. So far as I know I stand alone in the belief that it is feasible to wash puppies before they are six months old. Years of laundering them whenever they are dirty has never led to any dire results in our household. While the mother is keeping them clean, they are all right, but after she gets bored, puppies begin to look like lost children.

At this point I take a washbowl and Ivory flakes and a soft cloth and a pile of heated bath towels and a few doll sweaters. I dunk the babies in warm suds, massage them dry, put on the sweaters—and do they look enchanting! A solid black mite clad in a pink fuzzy doll sweater is something to write home about. If the air is at all cool, I put a warm hot-water bottle in a box with the babies and let them snuggle on it.

The idea is to keep the temperature so even that there is absolutely no shock. When the puppies are dry and clean, they look like fresh powderpuffs. They can be brushed with a soft brush.

Naturally, when you raise puppies in dozen lots or by the gross you can't spend your time bathing them, but if you have just a few, they may just as well be kept clean and no harm done.

At any rate, that's my story and I stick to it.

☆ ☆ ☆ ☆ ☆ 15 ☆ ☆ ☆ ☆ ☆

There are those who turn up their noses at dog shows. Particularly if they've never seen one. There are even benighted souls who say it is cruel to the poor little creatures to take them to shows. They remind me of the Hokinson cartoon in which a worn and broken lady looks at her treasure ensconced on a satin cushion in a basket and says, "I'm the one that should be lying down, not you!"

A spaniel in the show ring, eyes steady, head up, body posed, is about as smug as a prize-winning novelist. Spaniels love it. As for poodles, wirehairs, Pekes and Poms—it's almost indecent how they enjoy being the cynosure of all eyes.

The owners and handlers may mop fevered brows and prop their fallen arches up on crates and swallow aspirin. But the dogs don't need any sympathy. I often see handlers and owners exchanging pills. "Here, this will absolutely stop that headache." "Try this, you'll feel better." "Now, this is what my doctor gave me, it helps that pain when I bend over all day."

Meanwhile the dogs are in an elfin mood, prancing and primping and rolling seductive eyes at the ladies. Especially cockers love the ring. Nobody has to squeak mice at them or toss bits of liver in the air or rattle keys. They do their stuff for love and love alone.

Suppose you decide you have a dog that is not only the dearest, sweetest and so on, but also is a pretty fair specimen of the breed. The kind anybody would know was a cocker at first glance. Maybe it would be fun to show him. Not that you care a hoot about prize ribbons, certainly not, but just for the fun of the thing, the way people play bridge for the fun of it.

Dog shows are held all over the country and they are listed in the dog magazines, in the *Kennel Gazette* (A. K. C. publication) and in the voracious files of Mr. George Foley in Philadelphia. Mr. Foley runs licensed dog shows from practically sea to sea and sends entrance blanks at the drop of a hat.

Mr. Foley may be reached at 2009 Ranstead Street, Philadelphia 3, Pa., and a letter asking for entry blanks receives prompt attention.

Dogs are entered before the show, the blank gives a deadline date, and let me add, it is a deadline. You might more easily persuade the Income Tax Bureau to overlook a few days late filing than persuade the show list people to let your entry in after hours.

Any dog registered in the A. K. C. is eligible for

showing. A dog eligible for registration but not yet officially registered may be entered as "listed" on payment of a listing fee. For example, a dog from a registered litter that you have not yet individually registered may be shown "listed".

Your dog must be entered in a class and the official classes are usually: Puppy, Novice, American Bred, Limit, Open, Winners.

Puppy Class. Dogs six months, not over twelve months. The age shall be calculated up to and including day of show.

Novice Class. Six months and over, never having won a first prize at a dog show in any regular class except puppy class.

American Bred Class. All dogs (except champions) six months of age and over, whelped in the United States from a mating in the United States.

Limit Class. All dogs six months and over except champions.

Open Class. Any dog six months and over, except in a member specialty club show held only for American Bred dogs, in which case Open Class is limited to American Bred dogs.

Winners Class. Open to undefeated dogs which have won first prize in Puppy, Novice, American Bred, Limit or Open Classes.

Now you see you may be able to enter your dog in several classes, with the hope that he will earn points toward a championship or win blue in one class if he only gets red in another. The catch is, of course, you pay an entry fee for each class.

If you win in the winner's class, you get a trophy as well as a colored ribbon or rosette. The trophy becomes tarnished, the ribbon fades, but the points go on toward a championship.

Counting points is as confusing as figuring a golf handicap. Roughly speaking, sixteen points make a champion, the number of points at a given show depending on the number of entries and so on. It takes at least three 5-point shows under three different judges to make a championship and by that time you know all the rules anyway if your dog shows any signs of being a winner.

When you get to the show your dog is benched according to a number given on your entry card.

The official veterinary checks on the health, and all you have to do then is look in the catalogue and hunt up the dogs that are going to compete against you. They are all inferior to yours. But one of them will no doubt get the blue ribbon.

Once I met two ladies leaving a show with a cocker clutched in their arms. The cocker, half in one lady's arms, half in the other, looked dreamy and bland. One lady said in a choked voice, "Well, he may not have won a ribbon, but he's the most beautiful dog in the world to me!"

Getting a dog ready for the show involves a bit of expert dressmaking. The only way to know how to do this is to go to a show and hang over the ring all day, or sneak to the tables where professionals are grooming dogs. If I had a penny for each hour I have trailed surreptitiously after handlers, I could easily buy the Empire State Building.

With a duplex razor, scissors, barber's thinning shears, a good brush and a steel comb, you can practise on your dog. My early attempts involved borrowing my husband's razor while he was out of the house, but some men are fussy about their razors, and the duplex dresser works better anyway. Hair clippers such as barbers use, either hand or electric, do the best job of all on the head and neck.

Now the effect in the show ring should be a dog that is trim. The hair on the head should be shaved down until it lies smooth and even, with no extra fringe standing up like a cock's comb. The ears should be shaved down to look low and neat which means taking off any heavy feathering at the point where they join the head.

Whiskers come off and shaggy masses on throat also. If a dog has heavy shoulders they will look better trimmed down to give a smooth flowing line.

The feet should be trimmed by taking excess hair from between the toes and making a neat round of the foot. If the body coat is curly, the ringlets must come off to make the coat look smoother. The feathers are combed out and evened and if they grow thick on the front of the legs, these are trimmed off so the front will be straight and smooth.

Thorough brushing helps to give a look of tailored smartness, and a hound glove will smooth down a too-curly coat.

In the ring when the dog is posed, he stands firmly with front straight, head up, and the hindquarters drawn back a trifle to give a flowing beautiful topline. A cocker's hind legs should have a powerful angled thrust, and a correct pose will help if he hasn't as much angulation as he should have.

Always put your hand under the dog's body to pose him. Don't jerk him up and down by his tail which he is sensitive about.

The amateur in the ring will have as much difficulty behaving as the dog. Knees will shake, and hands quiver as you parade your treasure before the judge, but the calmer you seem the better. A nervous dog will have you on his mind, and be even more nervous. Never get between the dog and the judge if you can help it. Fortunately, the judge is not considering your points but the dog's.

The way to get the most satisfaction out of showing is to play for the game, not for the prizes. This is easier said than done, of course, when you and your particular glass of fashion and mold of form stand in the ring and watch that blue ribbon go to a dog put down by some famous handler.

If you can't take it with a smile, it is better to stay home. My own smile was pretty thin at one show when my ravishing darling went down before a knock-kneed and cross-eyed piece of fur and bones. I mean, those things actually do happen.

Most judging, however, is honest and as far as your showing is concerned, the judge must always be right. Begin with this premise and whatever happens, you will have fun.

For it is fun. An outdoor show under a soft blue summer sky with pennons flying, dogs barking, white-clad stewards running around like waterbugs, tents casting shade on the benches, sun in the ring, dogs and people surging over the clipped grass—this is fun. The smell of hamburgers, mustard, cool beer, steaming coffee, sawdust. People sitting on the grass opening picnic hampers while they talk about the show.

"And she had eaten all the buttons off my coat! I never thought I'd get her in the ring."

"No matter what the judge says, Nellie was the most beautiful dog in the ring. Look at her head! Look at her body! Look at her coat—"

"So there we were with five collies in the car, and the hotel objected to taking us! Three champions and two runners-up. I never was so mad in my life!"

"Five grains of aspirin is the answer."

Shadows lengthen. The judge drinks a glass of water in the big ring and watches the winners walk proudly before him. Who is the best in the show? There comes the little Papillon out of a doll's house, and there goes the Old English Sheep Dog, big as a bear, and you can't tell which is the front end or which the rear. The nervous beautiful Irish Setter moves along like a legendary prince in russet satin.

Silver trophies, brilliant ribbons, thunderous applause, and then all at once the dream fades. Station wagons roll away with Doberman Pinschers looking back from the windows. Crates are loaded in trucks with wire-hairs sniffing behind the mesh, scotties looking smug and wise. Three Great Danes drag a thin girl over the turf. The tents fall, the pennons go down.

Nothing remains except trampled grass and the light of sunset. Another show is done.

16

When I think about the ailments dogs are subject to, I feel as if I must rush out instantly and take the temperatures of the entire kennel. Dark memories of long nights, feverish anxiety, nameless terrors fill my mind. When death barks outside the door, one feels helpless, stricken.

A lady once asked me how long dogs lived. "Is twelve years a good age for a dog to live to?"

"Yes," I said.

"Then I don't think it's worth it," she said firmly. "Getting attached to them and all that—for twelve years."

I said nothing. I was thinking of my eleven weeks old puppy that died. I was glad I had her eleven weeks. Such happy weeks. If you must measure happiness in time, your lot is hazardous. In all things.

Dogs do get sick. People get sick. Flowers fade, candles burn down, birds leave the winter sky. That, unfortunately, is the way life is.

Nevertheless, there are a good many things you can do to make your dog live longer, to keep him healthy. Spaniels especially are naturally healthy, vigorous dogs and need the minimum of care to stay that way.

Given the right diet, exercise, and a clean dry bed a normal dog will be as rugged as the editor of a physical culture magazine.

A few general health hints may be useful. Long-eared dogs, such as spaniels, need care to keep the ears clean. A solution of bichloride of mercury in alcohol, in proportion one to one thousandth can be made up by any druggist. We keep a bottle beside the grooming brushes. Simple cotton swabs are made by wrapping a bit of sterile absorbent cotton around a match end (not the business end of the match).

When the dogs are brushed, we dip the swab in the solution and swab out the ears gently. Excess wax and dirt are taken out this way. It is possible also to use a medicine dropper and put in a few drops with it, rubbing the ears around with your hand afterward. Camphorated oil or even plain alcohol will do in a pinch.

There are other oil preparations which are good, also, but I think the solution of bichloride is really better, as it leaves no sticky residue in the ear canals.

Iodide dusting powder may be blown gently in by making a tiny cornucopia of paper, putting some powder in the horn and blowing through the other end. You don't need this for a good ear, but if any slight inflammation develops, it is healing.

If you consistently give your dog's ears this simple care, you can skip the next paragraph which concerns ear canker.

Spaniels are pushovers for ear canker; their long delicate ears invite it. When a dog shakes his head, scrubs it on the Aubusson carpet, ties himself in knots while trying to scratch with all four feet at once, whines, and generally carries on, the stop light is flashing.

You don't need the veterinarian's cute little light to reveal the pus and inflammation. You can smell it. If you lift the flap of an ear and take a whiff and meet a musty dark brownish odor, and then look in and see the redness in the outer parts of the ear, ear canker may be well under way.

Clean the ears out twice a day, being careful not to injure the delicate membranes by pushing the swab too deeply or with too much vigor. Dust boric acid powder or the iodide dusting powder in the ears. If it is at all possible take your dog to the veterinary.

Ear mites are parasites that you cannot see, but they are evidenced by scratching and rubbing also. A dark thick gummy material seems to be in the ear canals when the ear mites are settling down happily.

Drop ten drops of the bichloride of mercury in alcohol in each ear with the medicine dropper, and wipe the ears out with a dry cotton swab. Repeat this twice a week until the mites have gone to their fathers.

If the dog seems to have an earache, you may drop two drops of warm olive oil or glycerin in the ear, and give him an aspirin tablet. If it is the middle of the night, far from the doctor, fill a small, clean bag with salt and heat it quite hot and hold it to the painful ears. Put the baby to bed with it, so he can lie on the comforting warmth until sunrise.

Ear mites spread from dog to dog like lightning, so if your dog has been visiting friends and neighbors, clean out his ears and save trouble in case he has been exposed.

Another general suggestion is with regard to grooming. A dog that is brushed well, often, tends to have a healthy skin and a good coat. Dirt and dead hair never do anybody any good, and when a dog's skin becomes irritated trouble is in the offing. A good flea powder, well worked into the coat, will help keep fleas and lice from bedding down for the night. These powders now come in two forms, with or without DDT in them. The former is the more effective, without a doubt, but some dogs seem to be sensitive to DDT; so if you use it, check from time to time for any sign of skin irritation, and if there is even a trace, use the other type of powder.

There is still another type of powder, which we

use continually in our own kennel. It not only successfully combats parasites; it is a fungicide as well, and therefore actually prevents those types of skin disease which develop from a fungus infection. It is called I-F powder, and is available from the manufacturers of Life-Span products for dogs, who are the National Canine Products, Inc., 10 Franklin Street, Brooklyn 22, N. Y. It was developed under the supervision of our own veterinarian, and we were lucky enough to have had it during its experimental period. It has only recently become available commercially.

Always when you are bathing or dusting your Treasure, begin by massaging the suds or powder in a collar-fashion around the neck, then work down over the dog's body. This keeps fleas from moving up to the ears.

For spaniels, the ears should be combed or brushed on the under side first, then the ear turned over and brushed on the outside.

During summer vacation while you get a bad sunburn, Rover will undoubtedly get ticks. Ticks burrow in the skin and hang on with tenacity worthy of a better cause. You may feel their fat bodies protruding from your dog's skin, and the head and front feet or whatever else they have up front are buried nicely.

Pull them out very carefully. Half a tick left in will cause infection. A pair of small tweezers is a good instrument, wielded with care so the tick won't part company with itself but come out whole. If the beast hangs on very tightly, swab the spot with a drop of alcohol on a little cotton, and she will let go and can easily be removed. There are a number of insecticide powders which ward off most of the ticks. These differ in composition from the flea powders and have a peculiar musty odor.

A creolin bath will help keep down most skin pests. Two teaspoons of creolin to a scant gallon of water is about right. Or you can use a teaspoon of liquid nicotine sulfate to a gallon of water, and that, too, will get the best of both fleas and lice. If you use this last bath, however, make certain that the dog is very well rinsed before you dry him, as the stuff is poison.

Medicated dog soaps are all right, though few of them really kill parasites, and there is a dog shampoo which really gets all the visiting firemen, and furthermore keeps them away for some time afterward. I will tell you the name of it, although I am aware that trade names are taboo. It is called Cooper's Shampoo, and is made by William Cooper and Nephews, Chicago, Illinois. For some reason this has always been hard to get, and, at least for a time, it was very expensive; so we have been driven to trying out other shampoos. One of the best is Labco Pet Shampoo, put out by the Labco Pet Products Company, Boston, Mass. It kills fleas, lice, ticks, and their eggs, and is effective for several weeks afterward.

As far as I am concerned, these names are worthy of a place in the Social Register.

While your dog is busy getting ticks, he may also get weed seeds in his eyes. A teaspoonful of boric acid, dissolved in a glass of warm water, makes a fairly good eyewash, although I believe some dogs are unduly sensitive to boric acid. Yellow oxide ointment squeezed in the eyes is fine for most inflammation, if the seeds have irritated the eye. Vaseline may be rubbed on the lids to keep them from sticking together if no oxide is available. A drop of mercurochrome every other day may not add to your pet's beauty, but is a good antiseptic. This is only for an inflamed eye, of course.

Our standard remedy is metaphen in oil, as sold in drug stores. This will not irritate, even if the boric does, and it is good for a first aid for any developing eye difficulty.

Dogs have a third eyelid, called the Haw, which often becomes inflamed and protrudes like a small red football. Unless the swelling goes down in a day or so, the swelling must be removed, including the Harder gland which is on the inner surface of the third eyelid. An expert can clip the whole thing out and the dog will forget the affair in no time, and the operation is short and simple. But a poor operator can take out so much that the dog will always be subject to inflammation afterward, so try for a good doctor.

One more eye remedy, one which acts as an astringent on the blood vessels: ¼ per cent zinc sulphate in water (1 grain of zinc sulphate in 1 ounce of boiled water or boric acid solution).

Blond spaniels, or light reds often have dark streaks under the eyes—well, always do, if I must be frank. A little peroxide on a swab dabbed on the dark streaks helps, and also simply washing the streaks with water regularly.

The best way to keep the teeth clean is to give the dog good strong dog biscuit to chew. If the teeth are badly stained, they should be cleaned with gauze dipped in a mixture of two parts salt, one part pumice, two parts sodium bicarbonate. The dog won't care for this and will probably pack his suitcase and start for a sailing ship afterward, but you will have done your best.

Too much soft sloppy food is not good for the teeth. This is one argument in favor of a breakfast of pellets or kibbles not soaked in milk.

A change from country to city life may upset your dog a trifle. For grown dogs a tablespoonful of milk of magnesia given at night the first day or so will help regulate the bowels as he settles down to sedentary pursuits and forgets the rabbits he didn't catch.

17

The most talked of, and possibly least understood of all dog illnesses is distemper. It is a primary killer and crippler, it is the wolf that walks in the night. Distemper assumes so many forms and manifests itself in so many ways that it is like a horrible masquerade party. The symptoms are innumerable, the after-effects countless, and it strikes without warning.

Furthermore, it is so contagious that the germs may be carried in a person's clothes and live there for days.

The successful way to treat distemper is simply to prevent it. There are several ways of inoculating against distemper and a good veterinarian may safely immunize your dog with an inoculation so that you need never fear the murderous attack of this disease.

Don't put off having your dog inoculated. Don't wait until some other time. The inoculation is simple, and the dog will not suffer, and if he has a reaction, it is a minor one.

If you neglect this precaution, you may let your dog in for a dreadful illness and a painful death.

Between seven and twelve months of age is the period during which distemper strikes most often. But you can't be sure the dog won't catch it earlier or later.

Our own tragic introduction to the disease was typical enough to bear relating. We had a beautiful litter of puppies, sired by a champion, perfectly cared for, strong and vigorous. They were too young to have had their inoculation.

One afternoon we had a caller who was enchanted with the babies and played with them for an hour or so. When she reluctantly departed, she happened to mention these were the most beautiful puppies she had seen. "And," she added, "I spent all morning going the rounds of the pet shops, so I know."

Ten days later the puppies appeared to have slight colds, with running noses, and a little fever. They were listless and shivered now and then. Shortly they began to vomit and then they developed diarrhea.

The first beautiful dark red boy died in convulsions. Diagnosis—pneumonia. Distemper attacking respiratory system.

The exquisite little black female survived the original "cold" and lived to be eleven weeks old. Then she developed chorea. This begins with jerking of the legs or head and progresses into fatal convulsions. Diagnosis—chorea following distemper.

The black male grew more and more beautiful up to the age of eight months. Then he began with running fits and complete nervous degeneration followed including blindness. Diagnosis—destruction of the central nervous system following distemper.

One red male stuck it out and was left with only one mark of the beast, uneven ridges of enamel on the teeth.

We had learned the hard way. After this, nobody ever got in to visit our puppies until they had been protected from distemper. I find it possible to be rude to perfectly nice people who only want to cuddle one or two six weeks old puppies a few minutes. I find it easy to make callers keep their dogs in the car when puppies are in the yard.

I find it easy when I remember Red Boy and Donna and Tommy.

At the age of four months, inoculations are due. In other words, if you buy a three months' old puppy, have it inoculated by the next month, and meanwhile do not let him sniff around the lamp post, dig in debris in gutters, or romp with a dog in the alley. Never, never take him to see a friend who has a dog with a bad cold or a cough. Don't take him any place where there has been distemper in the building unless the disease has been over and done with at least three months.

I have a friend who makes a business of picking up stray dogs and getting them on their feet and finding homes for them. This is one of the most selfless occupations I can think of. What she does is nurse one case of distemper after another and too often she loses the struggle. Sometimes she wins.

Once a dog has distemper, the nearest doctor should at once be called to administer a dose of serum. This often checks the disease; it seems like a miracle when it does. The rest of the story is a story of nursing. Many apparently hopeless cases respond to patient nursing.

This is where your individual genius comes in. Some people are intuitive nurses with humans or dogs. They have a good chance of winning. As soon as a new symptom crops up, they will think of some way to fight it, and it would take an encyclopaedia to list all the trick variations they may face.

Intestinal trouble is one of the commonest forms of distemper. Diarrhea weakens the dog and every attempt must be made to check it.

For a sudden onset of diarrhea give two tablespoonfuls of castor oil to a grown dog, and this means scant tablespoons. If you and the dog spill a little, do not refill the spoon again. For puppies give proportionately less. Follow this by bismuth subnitrate 1 teaspoonful twice a day dissolved in water.

For acute diarrhea stop food for twenty-four

hours with the exception of small amounts of scraped raw beef.

Prolonged diarrhea with distemper requires systematic treatment, cod-liver oil, iron, plenty of raw beef. One capsule night and morning of "copperin A" for a grown dog is very helpful. Barley gruel is good also.

Keep the rectum clean with vaseline.

If the distemper affects the respiratory system, keep the nose and the eyes clean. Massage the chest with camphorated oil and cover with a light flannel. Be absolutely sure the temperature of the room is uniform, and the dog warm and dry.

If the distemper affects the nervous system, give sedatives, which I will discuss farther on.

Finally, do all your weeping outside where the dog doesn't know you feel sad. You can give a perfectly robust dog a headache by worrying over him, and a sick dog can't take any additional melancholy. Feed special tidbits by hand and make him as comfortable as possible, and promise him trips to Europe as soon as he gets well.

Keep all bedding clean, scald feeding bowls, sterilize spoons, put the roses out in the hall at night and send the visitors home when the hospital settles down for the night.

18

When you think your puppy is ill, run for the thermometer. Now, this business of taking temperatures is regarded differently by different individuals. For instance, I have a friend who takes her own temperature at the drop of the hat, and always knows whether it is point five or point four. When she is ill, she has only to remove the thermometer from her mouth long enough to tell you what degree of temperature she is running at that moment, and pop it back in again.

At the other extreme are the people like my mother. She never, for any reason, took her temperature. If she did have a fever, she felt, she might have to go to bed, but as long as she didn't check, she was able to keep on about her business and "throw it off." I have a dislike myself of actually getting a record of my temperature.

Then I have a friend who once threw her thermometer across the room and broke it because the mercury was rising instead of going down.

But a dog can't discuss his symptoms verbally and it may not be wise to wait for him to "throw it off." The little glass stick tells a lot.

STILLMEADOW SISTER

HONEY AND CLOVER WAIT FOR A SNACK

Normal temperature for a dog is 101 to 102 degrees. Usually 101.2 is what you should expect in a healthy dog, but some dogs normally register a little higher. But above 102, and if there is any sudden rise in temperature, you may believe your dog really doesn't feel like going to that party.

Remember that fever usually drops in the morning, rises during the day, and is highest at night.

To take the temperature, use a rectal thermometer, sterilized, and covered with vaseline. Insert it in the rectum about half the length of the tube, hold it there for about two minutes, and then brace yourself to read it. Never tell your dog what it is, lie cheerfully to him.

How much temperature he has, depends on the type of ailment.

In eclampsia, for example, it will climb blithely up to 106, by which time your own is probably around a thousand. Generally figures mean nothing to me, I ignore them. But those little numbers on the thermometer can make a lot of difference in my young life.

Five to ten grains of aspirin will help to bring down fever. For a puppy use half an aspirin dissolved in water in a teaspoon and masked with a pinch of sugar.

If your dog has not been immunized against distemper and runs a high temperature, suspect distemper immediately. You probably will be right.

Of course it may be only tonsillitis.

Whenever we have a sick dog in the kennel, we immediately isolate him and take the temperatures of *all* the rest. If they are normal, we feel sure the sick dog has some individual ailment and that the chances are no general infection is spreading. We then go into a huddle over just what Sister has been up to.

Clean and sterilize the thermometer immediately after using, and shake it down.

A sub-normal temperature frequently is found in distemper. Cover the dog well and keep him as warm as possible while the temperature is down.

19

Worms are the second horseman of the apocalypse. More puppies are carried away from this world of woe by worms than any other single ailment except distemper. A puppy with both worms and distemper hasn't even a fighting chance.

It is a curious fact that you may worm your brood matron when she is three weeks in whelp, keep her perfectly clean, feed only the best and cleanest food, wash her nipples with warm suds, bed the puppies down in clean newspapers, and the first thing you know, the little darlings begin to pass worms.

There are all kinds of worms, but there are four that lead in importance. Roundworms, tapeworms, hookworms, and whipworms are the common kinds. Hookworms and whipworms are fortunately less common than the first two types. They need a veterinarian for treatment, if you can get to one.

The first symptoms of worms in young puppies is that they *look* very fat but act lethargic. The stomachs are distended. They often gag or cough. Round worms, when passed or vomited up, are whitish rubbery looking things, rather unfortunately resembling uncooked Italian spaghetti. Tapeworms come out in flat small segments, and the head remains inside the dog while segments are expelled.

Dogs having tapeworm are not fat, but thin and poor looking. They eat ravenously and get no benefit from their meals.

The gums and inside of the mouths of dogs having worms look pale pink instead of red, and the dog is usually nervous. Anemia and rickets follow on the heels of the worms.

Examination of the stool by a veterinarian will determine the presence of worms and the kind. Lacking his helping microscope, you will often see evidences of worms if you look for them.

Never worm a dog that is sick unless the worms are so bad that you cannot possibly pull him along. Worming is drastic, and should be done with care.

There are a number of patent worm remedies on the market. So far as I know, there are two effective ones. The first is a form of tetrachlorethylene, and you might think the name alone would frighten the worms to death. This comes in sizes according to the body weight of the dog and should be used *only* by people who can follow printed directions to the letter.

All worm medicine should be given on an empty

stomach and followed in two hours by milk of magnesia, then by broth which is fat free.

The tetrachlorethylene remedy properly given to puppies will make new men of them in half a day. It gets both round and tapeworms. It paralyzes the worms and they are expelled rapidly. But they must immediately be gathered up and burned, or the puppy will be re-infected.

Also you must be careful the capsule does not break in the puppy's mouth. We have used this type of worming for years and had only one bad result. But that was a humdinger. My sister was in the puppy house quietly worming a batch of fat amber-eyed babies. I was in the house fixing flowers. Suddenly there was a scream and I looked out to see my sister doing a marathon to the house with a red puppy in one hand.

"It broke! He chewed it!" She kept screaming.

The puppy was already in convulsions and strangling. He seemed practically dying. Our first aid was instinctive, ours not to reason why, ours but to do or die. We sucked the worm medicine out of his mouth and throat. There was coffee on the stove. A spoonful of almost boiling black coffee was poured in the baby, followed in a moment by a spoonful of Scotch whiskey. Meanwhile we kept working his forelegs up and down, breathing in his throat, and wrapping him in a rapidly heated bath towel.

Next came milk of magnesia coating the mouth

to stop the burning. More whiskey. An electric heating pad. Coffee. In less than half an hour he was weaving around on my bed, drunk as a lord, and perfectly sound.

I merely tell this so you'll be careful.

The second type of medicine won't present this hazard, but it works over a period of three weeks, killing the worms slowly in their own stamping ground. It is a form of hexyresorcinol, also in capsules. If your puppy has a knot of worms obstructing his intestines, the first kind is indicated. If he only was a worm now and then, the second is used. We combine the two, giving the first for any serious infestation and the second as a general annual clean-up for all the dogs.

Very young puppies cannot be wormed. Usually eight weeks is the earliest date. But if you have an emergency, you may worm them successfully by drawing half the liquid from the smallest size capsule of the tetrachlorethylene compound with a hypodermic needle and giving the rest. The capsule will seal itself from the needle hole if it is held a moment in the hand. Don't try this if you are anywhere within miles of a veterinarian as it is an emergency measure only.

We once were given a present of a baby English setter. We didn't really need a baby setter with twenty-five spaniels and the neighbor's dog to take care of. But the poor little thing had just been knocked around from one person to another. So we took her in. She looked like a rat-catcher's dream.

We wormed her. It was all or nothing that time and it turned out to be all. If I told how many worms she had, nobody would believe it. It was incredible. She was nothing but skin and worms. In a couple of weeks no one would have recognized her. She was a happy romping girl with the world for her oyster.

Santinin may be used for very young puppies also. The tablets are cut in half and one-half given night and morning for a week. It's lots of fun and keeps you from worrying about the rent. Magnesia goes with it, half a teaspoonful.

A new product has been developed in recent years, which will eliminate round worms, and which is guaranteed to be non-toxic, and does not require that the puppy fast for hours before its use. It is put out by a highly reliable company, Lederle Laboratories, and is called Caricide. I suspect that in time it will replace the somewhat dangerous tetrachlorethylene capsules, where we have only round worms to deal with.

And finally, there is one old superstition that I have faith in. Garlic is good for worming. A clove of garlic cooked in the meat soup once or twice a week helps keep the kennel free from worms. Maybe the worms don't like the smell.

After the worming, give magnesia, a tablespoonful to a grown dog, less for puppies. If the worms are bad, an enema also helps clean them out. Veterinarians give a colonic irrigation for a thorough finish to worming.

As I have said neither milk nor meat gives worms. Filth and dirt help them breed and dogs pass them from one to the other with an uncommendable generosity. All bedding should be disinfected after worming, and we usually give the dogs a bath too, in case any eggs are left in the long hairs. Runs should be sprinkled with lime or bulk salt and thoroughly wet down and sunned.

20

Enemas may be used after worming, or in case of intestinal upsets. Constipation, gas, indigestion may be helped by enemas. One of our dogs once ate a lot of beach sand, why, Heaven knows. Another tried to digest a handful of straw.

Often an enema will help wash out any such stuff, and if the obstructive material is irritating, a mineral oil or olive oil enema is best.

I've spoken of obstruction due to knots of worms in the intestines. For this five drops of turpentine in eight ounces of warm water is the formula for the enema.

An ordinary run-of-the-mine enema is composed of a teaspoonful of soda in eight ounces of warm water.

Use the smallest tip available for the enema syringe and rub it well with vaseline. For small puppies we use an ear syringe filled with the enema solution and with the bulb squeezed slowly and evenly.

If a puppy strains and strains without results and humps miserably in the corner, he may have part of your coat button wedged in his little self. Try an enema.

In an emergency, rectal feeding may be resorted to. This is especially helpful for very young puppies that cannot get along without nourishment for long, and if they cannot take food by mouth they weaken rapidly. Give a preliminary enema of soda to clear the intestines and then a small amount of black coffee or beef extract, and hold the puppy on his side as long as possible so the stimulant may be absorbed.

Constipation may be due to a binding diet, change of scene, nervousness, or intestinal upset. Bone meal is constipating, as is too much meat.

For young puppies ten drops to a half teaspoonful of olive oil daily may be given.

Milk of magnesia is the best laxative you can use for man or beast. A teaspoonful for puppies, a tablespoonful for grown dogs. It is always safe to give magnesia if the dog seems ailing as it cannot harm him and is a mild anti-acid as well as laxative.

Castor oil should only be used in acute cases. I myself was brought up on it and think nothing of the stuff. With dogs, you don't have to put it in orange juice, but the after-effect is much the same as in children. It induces constipation as a reaction.

No patent human laxatives should ever be given a dog. Many of them contain ingredients that are absolutely poison to a dog's system, such as strychnine.

Mineral oil is fine, and for a case of chronic constipation may be given until the condition is corrected.

Canned mackerel or salmon, spinach, lettuce, chard, celery tops and tomato juice should be increased in the diet, and dry bread or toast omitted.

21

When your pet's crowning glory begins to fall out, it is time to tear your own hair. Skin diseases are not only bothersome to the dog, but they don't look pretty.

The soft deep glowing lustrous fur of a healthy spaniel is beautiful to see. But when the fur you love to touch begins to disappear in spots, you can't help being discouraged.

The earlier you notice any skin trouble, the better. Any sign of the hair being dry and lifeless and coming out in bunches, and any constant scratching that goes on should sound the warning bell.

Naturally if a dog is sick, his coat reflects his inner state. Worms, distemper, indigestion, anemia, affect the coat. Parasites irritate the skin and cause falling hair.

Then there is mange, of which there are various types. There is also eczema, and finally there is ringworm. These three are the common skin diseases, and if it is at all possible, you should enlist the aid of a veterinarian to combat them.

If there seems to be a mild general itching, rub

in the dog's coat a solution of two tablespoonful of powdered sulphur in a quart of hot water. Blanket the dog and let him dry without rinsing.

If there is dandruff, brush thoroughly until all dead hair and as much of the dandruff scale as possible is gone, then rub olive oil in the infected spots.

We have some solid blacks that get dandruff every winter while the buffs and parti-colors with them never have it. There appears to be a special sensitivity in the skin of the blacks, especially during cold weather.

If the dandruff is severe, we use a good hair tonic thoroughly rubbed in, or mange cure. There are a number of preparations advertised to keep the dog's coat in perfect condition, but so far as my own experience goes, a successful one has not yet been invented. The same mange cure used in barber shops is as good as anything.

If the dog has scratched too long and well and there are sores, wet or running, powder heavily with bismuth subnitrate or boric or stearate of zinc powder.

There are two kinds of eczema, dry and wet. In both, the hair falls out, the dog scratches like a maniac. In dry eczema the skin is scaly, in wet the patches rapidly assume the appearance of fresh beefsteak. The fur and skin just seem to be eaten away, leaving large expanses of raw dog.

One cause of eczema is undoubtedly diet, so

the first treatment should be to change the feed. Give plenty of cod-liver oil, meat, eggs, green vegetables, tomato juice.

Protect all raw spots from scratching. You can make a jacket which protects chest and hips, but it must fit snugly enough so that while the dog can walk, he can't sit down and work at himself.

Calamine and zinc ointment spread thickly over the sores and covered with gauze will clear up the wet type. For the dry, five per cent tannic acid and salicylic in alcohol is often effective.

Mange looks much like eczema. One type, follicular, is almost incurable, but fortunately this is rare. Only a microscopic examination can determine exactly which type is present. A shampoo and a good dousing with mange cure will help. Then rub olive oil or lanolin in the affected areas. The old-fashioned sulphur and lard is good if you haven't anything else handy. Stir powdered sulphur in the lard to make an ointment, rub it in well, and bandage the spots.

For patches of raw sore skin, paint the area with iodine once a day for two days, then skip two days.

Be sure to keep the bedding clean, and use plenty of chopped beef in the diet.

My notes on ringworm make very sad reading. The very word sounds like a knell in my ears. We had plenty of chance to make a case history of ringworm, for two of our favorite puppies caught it when they were away from home for a day.

Nothing would please me more than to tell just how and where, but I am going to control myself, and try to be a lady.

We first noticed small round spots on the muzzles, and a small spot on one boy's hind leg, on the top of his paw. The hair seemed to be wearing off from these spots. It didn't seem serious and I kept on singing around the house. I was still happy in my ignorance.

Little did I know what the next weeks would hold. The spots spread. We used our customary treatment for skin troubles. We changed the feed.

New spots appeared. Bigger and better spots. We decided it must be ringworm.

And it was. It took us almost a year to cure it, and meanwhile the two adolescent dogs had to be shut away from their companions, doused and blanketed, bathed and medicated. They spent half their waking hours in the bathroom and they lived in the midst of smells that must have made them wish they'd never been born.

Everything they got near had to be sterilized or burned, and that was no mean job. To this day, one of them won't stay alone in a room, lest he be shut up again and have ringworm. He has a good basis for his claustrophobia.

On that final day when the last vestige of ringworm disappeared, there was not a dry eye in the house.

My notes read like this:

Chrysarobin once per day. No good.

Iodex. N.G.

Iodine two days, skip two days. N.G.

Dr. A's prescription. N.G.

And so on, down to the last underlined remark —VERY contagious disease.

Finally effective was a remedy which has to be used with care as the dog can't eat it without being poisoned. Ten per cent ammoniated mercury ointment applied daily cured the ringworm. We used a small amount at a time and rubbed it in thoroughly to prevent the dog from licking it off. By this time the boys didn't lick anything off, they'd learned a lot in those hard months. If you use this, watch carefully, bandage spots where possible, and if the dog goes off his feed at all, stop the treatment for a day or so and hold the enemy at bay with mange cure.

Meanwhile be careful not to catch it yourself. I caught it. Iodine seems to work all right on humans.

I go into this fully because the grass is still green on my memory of the struggle, and if you recognize the first tiny ringworm, you may avoid all the difficulty by prompt, correct treatment. And any dog may pick it up if he is anywhere near it. It looks so innocuous, that little circle of bare skin.

Many times during our siege, we were near

giving up the sponge and the ship and anything else around that could be given up. But now when I see the shining silken soft coat on the dark red boy, I know it was worth it. He has lived to be a Beau Brummel, and to have litter after litter of rolypoly red boys and girls, soft as new butter and colored like sunsets' last fire. Even the black boy, who is nose down on some heavenly trail, had a time beneath the stars of magnificent freedom.

We have never had another case of ringworm. Maybe the gods decided we knew enough about it and should be graduated to the field of eclampsia.

22

When we bravely had our first litter, we assumed that when the puppies were born and settled down, the worst was over. The old Scotchman who owned the sire said, in passing, "Well, I hope the bitch doesn't 'fall over' on you."

"Falling over," we learned later, was what she did. She came down with eclampsia while I was taking a bath and there was a taxi strike in the city.

Eclampsia is an ailment of nursing bitches, and opinions differ as to the cause. One thing is certain, the primary cause is a litter of nursing puppies. Calcium deficiency is probably one factor, but we have had eclampsia with bitches practically running over with extra calcium from the date they were bred until the date they "fell over". Other bitches without calcium did all right.

Nervousness is another cause. I believe heredity has something to do with it. Certain sensitive, high-strung lines seem fated to have it.

On the other hand, a bitch may have it with one litter and not with another.

A large litter is supposed to bring it on, but we

have had eight in a litter and no eclampsia, and four in a litter with a dandy case.

Take your choice, and meanwhile, watch out for symptoms. Keep plenty of calcium in the diet and keep the bitch absolutely quiet and see that she gets enough exercise and isn't sitting in with the puppies every minute, night and day.

The customary first symptom is a nervous jerking of hind legs or body. A dry hard choking cough may announce the onset and you believe too readily that the bitch has got something stuck in her throat. One little mother who came down with it in the middle of the night left her babies and stumbled into my room and stood by my bed, actually telling me she was sick. She didn't bark or moan, but she uttered a curious desperate sound I have never heard before or since. But she was a dog with a very high I.Q.

If nothing is done to check the attack, convulsions will follow, the temperature begins to shoot, rising swiftly to around 106, and in twenty-four hours you may have a litter of orphans.

The attack is frightening, but if prompt corrective measures are taken, the bitch will soon be herself again, worrying about what private school the babies should attend next year.

The danger period for eclampsia is from fourteen to twenty-one days after whelping. Very rarely, a bitch may "fall over" in the fourth week. The sixteenth day seems to be our Waterloo.

The first thing to do when the bitch begins a nervous shaking or coughing is to take her away from the puppies. If the attack is mild, give two five-grain tablets of sodium bromide dissolved in water. Sponge the head and face with cold water and if she will take a raw egg and a cup of milk, so much the better. Keep her absolutely quiet, massage her legs and body gently. You may repeat the bromide in three hours if necessary.

Often you may prevent the eclampsia from being serious by this home treatment. During the first stages, you will notice the bitch panting as if she were in labor, her tongue will hang out, her eyes have a wild look. If your treatment is successful, she will gradually quiet down and go to sleep.

If the attack is severe you must get to a veterinarian as soon as possible, for time is of utmost importance in treatment. The veterinarian may give a massive injection of calcium gluconate with miraculous effect.

After eclampsia the bitch should be kept away from the puppies for gradually longer periods, you should increase the calcium in her diet as much as possible, and begin to give the puppies supplementary feedings as soon as they can manage to take them.

It is best to put her with the puppies briefly to relieve the pressure of the accumulated milk, then take her away and keep her as quiet as possible.

Whatever else is true of eclampsia, it is highly involved with mental and emotional factors. I noticed the arrival of noisy children in the house marked the beginning of one attack in our kennel. Confusion in the house from repairmen preceded another and, even more conclusive, the last attack coincided with a violent thunderstorm accompanied by terrific lightning and heavy crashes.

This gives another good reason for keeping visitors away from the litter until they are weaned, and the mother resumes her normal social life.

While eclampsia does not prohibit further litters for the bitch who succumbs to it, it is much better to be sure she is not bred again until she has had a good rest period and is in absolutely perfect physical shape. We always skip two heats following an attack.

23

Fits may be caused by a number of things, and may be relatively innocuous or extremely serious.

A friend of mine was in the middle of the main street in a city when her little black bitch suddenly had a fit, which caused a terrible commotion among the populace and worried the poor owner nearly into a fit herself. The worst of it was, they were taking a trip and my friend hardly knew whether to go home or go on.

This was a simple and obvious affair. The bitch was a sensitive aristocratic lady and she was upset at the strange town. The temperature of the place was, I believe, around a hundred in the shade and getting hotter. Moreover this particular dog never did like policemen and there were always policemen around on the corners. So quite understandably she had a fit.

The remedy in such a case is simple. Get the dog to a quiet place, preferably a darkened small room, the smaller the better, and let the fit work out. Bathe head with ice water, and when the dog can swallow give a nerve sedative. Feed lightly for the next few days but add as much vitamin B_1 to the diet as possible. Haliver oil capsules are good, also Beemax, Embo, Pablum.

Running fits may occur in puppies and frequently indicate lack of minerals and vitamins in the diet. They also may be an aftermath of distemper, in which case they may or may not grow worse. A high piercing scream generally precedes them, then the dog begins to race wildly around as if pursued by fiends.

Get the dog at once to a quiet dark place and give sedatives as soon as possible. During a severe fit, you can't give any medicine because the swallowing muscles are paralyzed. Cold cloths held over the head, cold water sponged gently on the muzzle help. Get him to a doctor as soon as possible after he is quiet.

If a dog goes into a running fit when he is excited about something, that is well and good. But if a dog is sleeping soundly and then goes into a fit, either running fit or regular convulsion, you may as well make up your mind that there is a serious neurological disturbance which in time may be fatal.

The dog is absolutely out of the world during a fit, and when he comes to, he will be dazed, tired, but without recollection of his seizure. You can then start building up his resistance and make sure that he has no worms, for worms may cause fits if they are present in any number.

Sometimes if you see a fit coming on, you can

ward it off by holding the dog in your arms in a dark room, bathing his muzzle gently and using all your charm to distract his mind and quiet his jumping nerves.

Chorea is a nervous disorder which is usually due to distemper. Spasmodic jerking, twitching, staggering fits, convulsions that increase in violence mark this disease. If it is a mild case, you may be able to save the dog.

Use the Fowler's Solution as listed under nerve sedatives.

NERVE SEDATIVES

Aspirin—5 to 10 grains for quieting effect.

Bromides—Non-effervescent triple bromides for a mild continuous effect such as for nervousness before a show. Three times a day. Do not continue too long as indigestion, poor appetite or bromide rash may result.

Sodium bromide—5 to 10 grains dissolved in water.

Fowler's Solution—in chorea conditions.

Day 1—1 drop twice daily
" 2—2 drops " "
" 3—3 drops " "
" 4—4 drops " "
" 5—5 drops " "
" 6—4 drops " "
" 7—3 drops " "
" 8—2 drops " "
" 9—1 drop " "

Stop 7 to 10 days and repeat.

Luminal—for restlessness without pain, carsickness, etc.

¼ to ½ grain for 3 months' old puppy

½ to 1 grain for grown dog

Morphine.

Nembutal.

Morphine and Nembutal are used only under a doctor's prescription. Both are dangerous unless used by an experienced person.

24

The first dog I ever had was poisoned. One of those fiends who enjoy the death of man's best friend laid out a meal of meat and strychnine for my dearly loved Brownie. That was years and years ago, and I remember as if it were yesterday Brownie dragging himself home to die in my mother's arms, looking pleadingly at her as if to apologize for being a bother.

A good many other dogs were poisoned at the same time, the town paper took it up and I believe the crime was finally traced to a man in our own neighborhood. But I remember all too vividly the grief that filled my heart day after day, and how my eyes swelled from constant crying.

The symptoms of poisoning often are stiffened hind legs, drawing up of the abdomen, moaning, bloody diarrhea. The dog will lie scrunched up with the head lower than the rest of the body and the hind legs drawn in.

Rush to the doctor, breaking all speed limits.

If you can't get a doctor and know what the poison was, give the proper antidote.

For immediate vomiting give mustard and

water, salt and water, ipecac by mouth. Try to produce vomiting.

After the vomiting give white of egg and milk, or milk of bismuth, which coats the intestinal tract and helps against absorption of poison and helps prevent burning. We always keep a bottle of milk of bismuth and if there is any suspicion of trouble, give a teaspoonful.

The first-aid rules are: First, induce vomiting; second, wash out stomach with fluid to dilute poison.

25

Food poisoning comes from decayed food, the lovely morsels of dead bird and rabbit the dog brings home. It is similar to human ptomaine.

To treat it, empty the stomach with ipecac, give castor oil, 2 tablespoonfuls for a grown dog. Stop all food for eight or twelve hours and then feed lightly beginning with broth and scraped beef and avoiding any starch such as melba toast or stale bread.

Do not try to stop a diarrhea from food poisoning for a while unless it seems too weakening. Nature is combating the poison herself.

Toxic poisoning calls for the doctor as soon as possible. A prolonged indigestion or intestinal stoppage may cause toxic poisoning. Fever, refusal of food, dull eyes, weakness are symptomatic of toxic poisoning.

If you can't get the doctor, give 2 tablespoonfuls of castor oil.

Or give five grains of salol and five grains of aspirin every three hours. The dose of salol may be doubled or tripled in a dire emergency.

Put 1 tablespoonful of dextrose in the drinking water, and give peptonoids by spoonful every hour or two for food. When the dog will eat, give only broths, raw eggs and milk in very small quantities.

Abscesses may be treated at home, if the veterinarian is unavailable. Wait until there is a soft spot in the center of the hard mass. Shave the hair away, paint with iodine.

Sterilize a small sharp knife and a small sharp pair of scissors by boiling twenty minutes. Grit your teeth and make an incision through the skin and press the pus out, squeezing as much as will come.

Use sterile iodoform gauze to pack gently in the opening as a drain, letting one end hang out. Soak a wad of cotton in Dakin's solution or normal salt solution (1 teaspoonful salt to 1 pint of water) or water to which a few drops of iodine have been added.

Bandage the whole and keep the bandage wet with the solution. Change the drain and bandage in 48 hours, again in 48 hours until the wound is healing and no sign of pus remains.

The treatment for boils is much the same. Boils are a sign of poor blood and the diet should be reinforced with cod-liver oil, irradiated yeast, calcium. When the boil comes to a head, lance it with a sterile needle or razor blade and wash with disinfectant. Give milk of magnesia to clear up the bowels.

Boils don't need to be bandaged.

26

Mad dogs and Englishmen go out in the noonday sun, according to Noel Coward. He implies that there is no cure for either, and he is correct about the first in any case.

Rabies is incurable. The rabies inoculation is a preventative, but not a permanent one, and the great advantage of it is the little tag which you hang around your dog's neck so that nobody will shoot him if he begins to snap at a Bedouin camel going down the street on the way to the circus.

Every now and then there is a rabies scare. Policemen go about potting any dog that is barking or isn't barking. People who don't like dogs suspect rabies at the drop of the hat.

A dog that is terrified by having sticks thrown at him and being yelled at and chased around can stage a fine imitation of frenzy. Who wouldn't?

Everybody knows the symptoms. Scareheads in newspapers keep them in the public mind. Rabies is a virus disease and the virus is present in the saliva of the infected dog, whence it is passed on by a bite. The saliva will also infect if it comes in contact with a broken place on the skin.

The Pasteur treatment must be taken at once by humans who are exposed to rabies by either of the above ways.

Many states require the rabies inoculation for your dog, so if you are embarking on a tour with him, get the inoculation first and save any possible trouble, and carry the certificate with you.

The best way to combat rabies either real or fancied, is to co-operate with the A.S.P.C.A. in keeping stray dogs off the streets. England has eliminated the disease altogether through rigid quarantine laws and elimination of loose running strays.

Meanwhile, if you keep your dog from roaming, don't let strays invite him to tea, and keep him on a leash in the city, you can dismiss the old bogey from your mind. He won't catch rabies out of the air like a butterfly. He won't get it from meat, milk, water, or hot weather.

27

Accidents will happen. When I was very young, after I had made rabbit trails all over the house with talcum powder, I said, "But, Mamma, you never told me not to make rabbit tracks with the powder!"

"Nobody could think of everything ahead of you," said my poor mother, in despair.

Dogs are much the same. They can think of a lot of things quicker than you can. Especially puppies. They can get caught in a revolving door, eat buttons, munch soap, suck up feathers, try to play with fish hooks and so on ad infinitum. My favorite tale is of the dog that ate twenty-nine pieces of bathroom tile.

Once a wild scream brought me to the lawn where Rendezvous was having a rendezvous with a pickerel lure. The lure had nine hooks, but Ronnie was the only fish ever caught on it.

Charming Tranquillity got her teeth stuck in a fence wire and couldn't get away. Sister once consumed half the arm of a chair. Rip found a wasp nest.

STILLMEADOW HILDEGARDE C.D.—STILLMEADOW HERITAGE C.D.X.

STILLMEADOW SAXON

My Irish setter got his muzzle peppered with porcupine quills.

Sitting down in a fresh paint can is a dandy game.

About the only thing they don't do is climb trees and get marooned there, and that isn't their fault. It's just because they can't climb. I had two gray kittens once that had to be picked regularly as raspberries, but they were higher up; they ripened in maples.

In case of accidents, you have to rely on your native intelligence. Porcupine quills must be removed carefully with pliers or forceps, as the barbs are very dangerous. Then iodine must be dabbed on the wounds.

Fresh paint should never be cleaned off with turpentine. The dog will go crazy and so will you. Wipe off what you can remove, and let the rest wear off. Don't let the dog lick it—lead is poison.

Strains or pulled tendons should be tightly bandaged with gauze and fixed on with adhesive, the gauze I mean. Whenever you use adhesive, try to make most of the bandage of gauze and anchor it at edges with adhesive, so that you can cut it away without hurting the dog later on.

Cracked or cut pads should be soaked in disinfectant and painted with iodine, and bandaged if the cut is deep.

Wounds from arguments with other dogs should have the surrounding hair shaved away and be cleaned out thoroughly with disinfectant. Usually bleeding stops of its own accord and it is safer not to bandage unless you have to.

Strong tea is the quickest burn remedy. Follow it by spreading oil or a burn ointment over the burned area.

Broken bones should not be treated at home. Get the dog to a doctor if you have to fly to Timbuctoo to do it. And keep the dog as still as possible on the trip. Use nerve sedatives.

Obstructions in the throat may be taken out by holding the dog's jaws apart and thrusting two fingers down and drawing out the what-is-it, being careful not to tear the throat tissues. If the obstruction is too far down, give mineral oil repeatedly to grease the progress down.

Once in the stomach, bone fragments or fish bones will dissolve. Beads and buttons will not. If the dog swallows an elephant, you will have to get the doctor to use the fluoroscope on him to see how much of the elephant is there.

The worst accident we ever had was when Star was on her way to the neighboring town with me. A dog across the road rushed at her as she was getting in the car, and tore one eye out.

I had supposed that I had lived through everything a human could, but I was certainly wrong. The trip with Star, eighty miles to the Miller Cat and Dog Hospital in a driving rain, while Star and

I and a profuse hemorrhage kept a kind of death watch—well, that trip was something.

So now I know what to do in such an emergency, knowledge so dearly bought that I would pass it on.

Make a boric acid compress and lay it on the whole side of the face, eye and all, trying if possible to keep the eye back in place. Bandage the compress in place, and ride for the doctor.

The sight will be gone, in any case, but if you can save the eyeball, the dog will live to forget the whole thing. If the whole eye has to be removed due to infection, the empty socket will catch dust and dirt and be a constant irritation unless the surgeon sews the eyelids together. Actually this looks a great deal better, too.

Fortunately Star's eye was correctly treated, and now as she races over the lawn after a ball, nobody would know that she sees it only with her one good eye. She doesn't know she has a handicap, and I don't even think she sits around the fire at night saying to the other dogs, "Now when I had my operation—"

That is one superior thing about dogs, by the way. They don't carry their past ailments along with them and re-hash their aches and pains. What's done is done. They begin again with no backward sniff. There's always a new trail ahead.

28

Any discussion of ailments is apt to make one feel that a dog's life is literally that. You may feel that it is true they never have hair-balls, like cats, but they are heir to everything else under the sun. But actually a dog, especially a spaniel, is a naturally healthy and easy-to-care-for little animal.

No one dog has everything; some dogs never have even a cold in the head. And all the dogs will never have the same ailments at the same time, And, too, the March of Science is even overtaking many formerly fatal enemies. New techniques, discoveries such as the sulfa drugs and the light-ray treatment for parasites, which sounds so much like a fairy tale, these are narrowing the field of dog ailments.

Research develops new treatment for skin troubles, colitis, dietary allergies and so on.

The fact is, it is only reading over a medical article that depresses one unduly. It is hard to go over an entire catalogue of possible ailments, and not succumb to a nervous state bordering on the frantic.

We have a book in the country on First Aid for

humans. Theoretically it should be a comforting tome, a bulwark against difficulty. But I well remember the first, and the only time I consulted it.

I had a rash on my hands and I wondered whether it could be poison ivy. (It was.) I bounded up the stairs and found the tome of medical aid under the developing tank in the bathroom.

I sat down and began to leaf through the pages, expecting great comfort. I followed the listing.

Fever. Fracture. Fits.

I began to feel very odd. I felt feverish. My bones ached. I read on. Snake bite. I had shooting pains in my ankle where a snake might have bitten me.

By the time I got to the description of rigor mortis, I had that too. I was myself a complete dictionary of accident and disease. I had just sense enough in the end, dizzy and weak as I was from my bout with the voice of experience, to close the book and totter feebly back downstairs.

The one thing I actually had, and how I did have that thing, wasn't mentioned at all in this particular encyclopaedia.

Well, that settled that. I decided never to look at that book again.

Now this same thing is very apt to happen to a nervous and sensitive dog owner. If the dog has a symptom of any kind at all, you may talk yourself into believing he is running the whole gamut of ailments. I have known people with dogs as strong as the Rock of Gibraltar who were continually worrying their heads off because the dog seemed not to act quite right. He drank too much water, or he didn't drink enough water. He was too cold, or too hot. He ate too well, or didn't touch his last meal.

Now a dog has moods, even as you and I. No dog wants to be bright and the life of the party every single minute. Once in a while, he may even wish to sit and think about how everybody misunderstands him.

He will react to any family troubles, too. He is conscious of the fact that Papa is in a terrible mood and Mamma is ready to go home and lead her own life. He may sit dejected and hopeless and refuse to eat if you have been crying your heart out over your own problems.

He is also responsive about himself. If you ask him tenderly, "Does your poor little head ache?" His head will ache, all right. What a headache!

The best course to follow is to be ready for an emergency and then go on and enjoy life with your merry little companion.

For the benefit of people who don't live over a drugstore or with a fleet of high-powered cars drawn up at the door ready to do errands, I am putting in a list of minimum medical supplies. Even if you have only one dog, it is a good thing to have a medicine shelf or cabinet for his supplies. If you like gadgets you can always add them, just as you may buy pajamas, lace-edged panties, and galoshes, if you want them for your darling. I myself yearn over turquoise-studded collars, but never have had one.

If you are raising a puppy or a litter, you should get a camera and take snapshots for a permanent record. A puppy is cutting teeth one minute and the next is ready to set up a house of his own.

Apropos of this, be sure the collar isn't too tight. The neck size changes, but I have seen dogs practically strangling with the same collar they wore when they were in kindergarten.

A harness is not advisable. It stretches the shoulders and pulls the dog in wrong places. A round, not flat, collar is the best possible, and a leash that is not so heavy as to drag down.

29

This is the list for the medicine cabinet for the head of the house.

General—
  Boric acid
  Bicarbonate of soda
  Absorbent cotton
  Adhesive tape
  Gauze bandage (2-inch width)
  Swabs (wooden matches will do)
  Iodine (2 per cent solution)
  Mercurochrome
Laxatives—
  Castor oil
  Olive oil
  Milk of Magnesia
Emetics—
  Dry mustard
Sedatives—
  Aspirin (5-grain tablets)
  Sodium bromides (5-grain tablets)
Skin medication—
  Powdered sulphur
  Cooper's Shampoo or Labco Pet Shampoo
  Glover's mange cure

168

Ears—
 Bichloride of mercury in alcohol, 1 to 1000, or
 Camphorated oil
Eyes—
 Yellow oxide of mercury
Worms—
 Tetrachlorethylene capsules, or
 Caricide

Please note that this list is for people who hole in far from the madding throng. City folks don't need anything on their shelves except milk of magnesia, because the druggist is nearly always keeping open house. But in the country, you roll your own, so to speak, and it's better to have everything you need than to find out that you lack just that one bottle or box which will fix your dog up again.

A complete medicine supply is not expensive, and most of the listed items will keep until you need them.

We house the grooming equipment nearby, and next to that dry dog food, dry cereal, canned meat, evaporated milk, and bone meal and cod-liver oil.

Brushes, combs, and scissors should be sterilized frequently, and a separate set used for any dog with a skin disease.

If you are raising puppies, you need a small kennel file for the individual records, papers, registrations, and so forth.

You can aways have special cabinets built for silver platters and bowls and other utterly useless but shining trophies.

30

"Roger is a perfectly darling dog," says the lady on the end of the leash, but he just will bite the milkman. What shall I do?"

"Miranda doesn't like to be left alone," says Mrs. Smith, "so she always tears up all the lamp shades when I leave her. What do you suggest?"

If I tried to list all the things dogs can do that make trouble, it would use up a freight car load of paper.

For dogs have as many personality traits as people. And if you think all dogs should be perfect all the time in behavior and temper, look around you and find a flawless person in your group. If you find one, you will be very glad to get back to the imperfections of Bingo or Champion Honeygold's Best Bet.

Personality problems may arise from a number of causes. If there is too much inbreeding, nervous and timid and high-strung dogs may be the result, along with those beautiful heads, compact bodies, elegant coats. Because you can't have everything.

Your dog may inherit a special personality, just be born a certain way. Then you may always eye him fiercely and say, "You got that from your mother!"

Then there is environment. Take a litter of puppies and raise one in a big commercial kennel run, another in a penthouse, a third in a grocery store, a fourth in the upstairs bedroom, a fifth on a farm. Now all those puppies will have certain characteristics that are alike, but also they will differ so much that you might not know they were second cousins once removed by the time they are grown and running their own households.

Environment includes the owners. The first question to ask if your dog has any personality difficulty is "What have I done?" You may be surprised.

At first we couldn't understand why Honey took ten minutes to come in the back door and then scurried in looking behind her as if the Valkyries were winging past. Then we found that someone had slammed the door on her, just once, and frightened her out of her senses. The rest of her life, Honey has been careful about doors, and I have caught many a cold standing with the door open on a dark winter night while she sidles up, peers, backs away, and finally enters. Or in summer, waiting while all the flies and wasps in Connecticut precede my darling!

Again, the reason we raise what could be called window sill cockers is due simply to the fact that they grow up seeing the cats leap from pillar to post, and they do their best.

A dog that shies away from his owner is pretty apt to be a dog that has been whacked when he came up one time or another. The hand should never be a weapon of punishment, it should only be used for petting and praise. If you want to beat your dog, at least use a folded paper or a magazine. Better still, give him away and get the whole thing out of your mind. You could try a bird, which will never get underfoot or open the special delivery package for you and eat the tag.

In many ways, dogs' senses are so much more acute than ours that often something which affects them violently may not even be noticed by what we call our superior intelligence. I have seen a dog break in an obedience test because he felt the line of folding chairs was so close, it might collapse on him. The owner never even saw it.

Then there is that little matter of health. We are familiar enough with the swamps of depression we get into after a high temperature with flu. We know that an upset stomach can make a perfectly nice husband temporarily a fit subject for the Bronx zoo. All the ills the flesh is heir to affect the spirits and temperament too. A child who is a little anemic seems listless and indifferent. And as for that hapless thyroid gland, what it can do is nothing short of amazing.

Yet how seldom do we wonder whether our dog

may have some physical basis for a snapping fit or for an hour spent ripping the bedspread to pieces?

It was not until I had raised dogs for many years that the discovery burst on the world that a deficiency in diet or a vitamin deficiency could cause upsets in the personality.

A dog that develops sudden crotchets may need a prescription from your drugstore. The complexes of vitamin B, for instance, are often helpful with nervous conditions. Calcium lactate may improve the dog's health.

For even though your dog may get a perfectly balanced diet, his own system may at some time need an extra amount of one kind of nutriment or other, and adding that plus value may bring him to the peak of condition.

It is an old story that worms make a dog cranky. I think a good deal of unnecessary snapping is due to worms. The dog doesn't know what to do about the feeling he has, he wants to react, and he snaps. Maybe he snaps at a visiting fireman, and that is your hard luck.

What this all adds up to is that when your darling sits brooding in a corner or runs around acting like a juvenile delinquent, your first job is to check his social environment for anything no civilized dog should put up with, and then to check his health.

One woman I know had a little Boy Scout cocker who suddenly became so vicious that she was told that she must put him to sleep. But careful investigation of the background made the trouble plain. Really her mother-in-law was the one who should have been put to sleep if a just judgment were rendered.

The cocker and his owner had moved in with mother because of the war. Buddy was suddenly moved from a happy home to a strange place where everything he did resulted in "Bad dog! Dirty dog!" and plenty of slaps when his mistress was out at work. He and mother were alone most of the day, and she simply hated dogs.

So, in the end, he bit her.

This sad story is repeated in different degrees in many cases. Frequently if there is help in the house, the dog may get in the way now and then. He has feeding dishes to wash and fresh water to be put down. He is, in short, a nuisance, and he may be told so all day long by the help. And, above all else, a dog needs security. Especially Spaniels need it, for love is the key to their whole existence.

It is unfortunate that it is so easy to take out any bad temper on the dog. If the soufflé falls, and the ironer rips off all the shirt buttons, and the bathroom pipes begin to leak and just at that minute, Bunny turns up with a filthy gangrenous old bone and gets on the bed with it—well, Bunny may get punished not only for that bone but for the soufflé and the buttons and the pipes. Which shows what an unjust world we live in.

Now it is perfectly possible for a dog to be really mentally ill. It doesn't follow you should go around saying "All Spaniels are crazy," but that is the way people usually do.

The type of distemper that attacks the nervous system may affect the dog. Chorea, the jerking of the head or legs, or a partial paralysis is an obvious aftereffect. But sudden snapping or biting fits may also be due to that old killer distemper. If the dog turns on the person he loved most in the world, there is reason to suspect he is a victim of distemper nervous disintegration. Particularly if between the attacks, he is his old loving self. And if he is quietly sleeping and starts up and rushes to bite someone, it is a pretty definite sign of trouble.

The prognosis for this type of mental disturbance is very bad. If your dog has a history of distemper, and if you have checked all other possibilities, consult your veterinarian, and if he so advises, put him to sleep. For he is suffering more than you from the trouble. And the condition will grow worse.

For personality problems which have no physical basis, there are many and varied remedies, but not as many nor as varied as the problems.

"Ruffles has a bad habit," says one distracted owner. "She sneaks in the bathroom and gets an end of the toilet paper and then runs all over the house trailing it after her. If we are having company for dinner, it is really embarrassing."

Well, you could think a long time before you would come on that one!

Then there is Rob Roy who runs away so much that a standing ad is in the paper for his return. Rob Roy is not alone. Setters are typical wanderers, but cockers can also like to pack their bags and go for a weekend jaunt.

Then there is Sugar N' Spice who decides she will only eat broiled steak. That's a personality problem too. You can always sit down with her and tell her about Snow White and the Seven Dwarfs while she eats her chopped beef and vegetables, or you can train her, or you can give her the steak. It's up to you.

"My three little cockers get up on the table and help themselves whenever I leave the room," says Mrs. G. "They are so energetic and bright, the little darlings!"

And so they are. Much brighter than their mistress.

I would be the last to say that Stillmeadow cockers behave as if they were in Sunday School all day long. But I can say that the younger ones behave better than the first ones we raised. With years of practise, I have become, I hope, a better owner, and the resulting behavior of the cockers is far, far better.

How I wish I could pass on everything I have

learned, all done up in a capsule in a small bottle labeled, "Take before you get that puppy!"

Or perhaps I should put it up in three capsules.

1. Begin establishing the right habits.
2. Teach your puppy the word NO.
3. Increase your mutual understanding by Obedience Training, if you can get it, but training in the home at least.

☆ ☆ ☆ ☆ ☆ 31 ☆ ☆ ☆ ☆ ☆

I MENTIONED Obedience Work in connection with the training of your puppy. And I spoke about the thrill of my first obedience show. At that time, I was an innocent spectator, and I sat at the ringside. I complained a little about how hard the folding chair was and little did I realize, as the Victorian novels would say, little indeed did I realize how fortunate I was to be sitting, no matter on what.

A year later I was inside that ring with Little Sister and my aching feet had fared many a mile. I had a crick in my neck from peering down to see whether she was heeling correctly. My hands were numb with nervousness, and I was peppered well with mosquito bites from our last dress rehearsal in the yard the night before.

But when I stood in line and gathered in a red ribbon and a small and utterly useless silver candy dish, and Sister sat so smugly with the laurels around her little dark head, I wouldn't have changed places with the owner of the Empire State Building.

And so, for the benefit of dog owners who are

really willing to give up considerable time for the training and who do not care a fig for fallen arches, stiff backs, sunburn in summer or frostbite in winter, I would like to discuss Obedience Work a little more fully.

In this country, it is fairly new. Mrs. Whitehouse Walker, of Bedford Hills, New York, was the pioneer and the year was 1934. In England it is much older. In this brief time, classes have sprung up all over the United States, and most shows include Obedience trials as well as breed exhibiting. The American Kennel Club regulates the shows, and issues the certificates to the successful candidates for degrees.

A good many dog clubs give informal match or sanction shows where you may try your wings without the strain of a big time show. These also are run with kennel club rules, but you do not win points toward the degrees. You have the practise of working under a judge and you may win a bag of dog food or a box of writing paper, and if everything goes well, you have a wonderful time.

Now just what does Obedience Work involve?
Patience and work.

The rewards are countless, but let's face the fact that it does mean work. But most good things do, I find.

For instance, it is wonderful to speak a foreign language and to read great literature in its native tongue. But first you struggle wildly with all those little sentences about "My aunt is sitting in the arbor" or "The general has gone to war, but the queen stays home."

Obedience Work is much the same. You and your dog are establishing a mutual vocabulary, you are really learning how to communicate with him, and he is learning a whole new language. So you can't expect it to take an idle hour or so.

And I think this should be made plain at the outset. In our classes, there are always people who come in one session, lose their temper when Sidney does not perform perfectly, and never come back. Their dog is just no good, they say. Very often the veteran members will speak softly to one another behind their dumbbells.

"That would be a good worker," they say, "if only he had a decent handler."

Well, how much patience and how much work?

This depends on the individual dog, and a good deal on the ability of the handler.

For there are some dogs that are slow and stubborn, and there are some people who will never, never be able to teach their dog what to do. Some people can never learn to play the piano, and some people just can't cook, and some people can't train a dog.

I know one amiable and competent little cocker who made miraculous progress with his handler. The class used to stand with eyes popping out while Peregrine whisked through the most advanced exercises. And then the handler had to turn Peregrine over to another member of the family, on account of being ill. And in a few weeks, you would say the cocker was really a hopeless case. He just couldn't keep his mind on anything. He even forgot how to heel in the course of time.

Generally speaking, cockers learn quickly. But it takes time to steady them down. It is better not to set a definite time, but to work along until you feel confidence that your dog will not break, will perform creditably. If you are not training him for a show, or for a degree, it is still better to let him learn one set of commands thoroughly before you move on to new ones. I have seen a wonderfully intelligent little cocker completely confused and set back by his handler's ambition to have him do the utility exercises before he had the novice work firmly in his eager little mind.

Is it worth all this effort?

I must try to restrain my enthusiasm. I will only say conservatively and modestly that Obedience Work is the most wonderful, most exciting, most rewarding, most satisfying—well, you get a dim idea of how I feel about it.

Now Obedience Work, as I have said before, and will say many more times, has nothing to do with tricks. When you and your dog have learned Obedience Work, you understand each other. Your companionship is increased a hundredfold, for now on top of all your love and friendship you have the old school tie! You have studied, practised, passed your examinations, won your degrees together. And it is this enlarged horizon which you share that is the greatest reward.

An educated dog is better than an ignorant dog. It is a great waste, especially for Spaniels, to idle life away. A cocker is much happier if he can use his intelligence.

Further, a timid dog gains security and stops sneaking under the bureau when the doorbell rings. A dog that bites milkmen will greet them with a kind smile. A spoiled bouncing pet will keep off the guest's white silk frock. I will go right on out on that legendary limb and say that Obedience Work will help any personality difficulty unless it is based on a physical illness. It may not make a democrat out of an anarchist, but it will help!

Practically it helps too. It is fine to have your dog come when you call him and stay where you ask him to. You may not always have time enough to chase your little sugar pie all around the yard when you want him to come in to bed. It is nice to have him polite to dog-hating visitors. It is convenient to take a walk with him on a crowded city street without being wrapped around the lamp posts and hauled breathlessly back and forth. It is pleasant to have him sit, stay beside the tea table until his own plate of cookies is served, instead of having him lean his elbows on the table and go over all the cookies with a moist nose.

And it isn't really cruel of you, for you can take him to other houses for other teas when he is a gentleman and he will be quite welcome.

All of these advantages come in the novice training.

With the advanced work you may get more spectacular results. We all have heard of the man who lost his auto keys on a walk in the woods. He had his utility trained dog with him, and he simply sent the dog back for the keys. The dog brought them in a jiffy. He was doing the scent discrimination exercise for the metal object!

Now and then a dog's life is saved because he will drop at the sight of his owner's lifted hand. The auto passes on, or the fighting dog is dragged away, and he is alive and unscratched.

But you don't have to have a five alarm fire to enjoy the benefits of your training. Every day is better with your alert, steady, well-behaved Companion Dog.

In the obedience classes, you will find all sorts of breeds. And it is extremely beneficial for your cocker to learn how to get along with Shepherds and Dobermans and Danes and Dachshunds. He may be afraid of the big dogs at first, and when his fear vanishes, he feels pretty proud of himself.

He will from now on be able to go anywhere and meet any four legs without screaming woof, woof and flying to your arms. For he knows no matter how peculiar the creature may seem, it is just another dog such as he lies down with in school!

We began our training with Melody because she was one of the most difficult charming little cockers we ever had. Melody is a beautiful solid black with an eager face and a quick sense of humor. She is passionate, intense, stubborner than ten mules, dreadfully jealous, and by nature a chaser of cats.

Besides that, she always flew to the farthest corner under the range when visitors came or when she was supposed to go outdoors. She was perfectly housebroken, unless it rained outdoors.

In other words, we loved her madly, and she was a very poor member of society.

"If she can be trained," we said, "anybody can."

And the day Melody skipped across the ring in a driving rain to complete her Companion Dog degree, I wasn't the only one who wept with joy and excitement.

Now Melody loves company. She adores going to shows. She is the life of the party. She keeps her jealousy down to a low mutter when someone else is in that favorite lap. She goes out when she is told to, she even goes in the kennel when it is her turn to spend the night there.

But it took six weeks to get her to Sit on command. And the first night she went to class, she bit a large and earnest Shepherd who was merely passing by!

So there was no abracadabra about it.

"But if I join a class and go once a week," said a friend of mine, "Buffy will be trained." She added, "I don't have any time to practise her at home. I'm busy."

"So are we all," said the trainer. "Lots of us work nights part of the week too. You can find fifteen minutes a day. Anybody can."

Unfortunately the laws of education apply to Obedience, and you have to do homework ten or fifteen minutes a day at least.

There are Obedience classes in many parts of the country now, with more being established constantly as interest rises. You can train your dog at home alone, but a class helps immeasurably, and if you want to get that degree from the American Kennel Club, you need the classwork before you enter the grueling competition in the show ring.

If you can go once a week to a class, and give that fifteen minute training period a day, you will get results.

"I don't care anything about degrees," people always say when they begin. "I just want to get Phillip to come when he is called."

In the course of time, Phillip can be seen coming in on the recall and sitting in front of his mistress, then heeling smartly on command.

"I wonder if he would qualify if he did go in a show?" the owner says wistfully.

And the next thing you know, there comes

Phillip heeling into the show ring on a hot summer's day.

Now there is one thing I want to make clear before you even start. You do not train your dog by abuse or fear. If you want to whack your dog around, you had better stay at home. You train your dog with patience and love. If you cannot control your temper when he makes a mistake, you do not belong in Obedience Work at all.

Having visited every class anywhere within reach over a period of several years, I will admit that there are trainers who think you may as well let your dog know you are the master and that a spike collar is a fine training aid.

I hasten to add I do not know of any classes in Connecticut which are run on that basis—which may be one reason the dogs do so well in the shows.

"Always make sure your dog enjoys the work," says my favorite trainer. "It is fun for you both. Never forget that. Praise him lavishly. Keep his confidence all the time."

This is sound psychology, just as it is for children—or adults.

With cockers, it is particularly important. Cockers are sensitive to the very tones of your voice. Frighten your cocker and he will pack up his grip and go home. Work with patience and an even discipline, and he will jump with joy when the collar comes out.

At Stillmeadow, with five dogs in training, we resort to all kinds of dodges to keep it a secret when one goes out for practice. All the rest go into a decline, nursing broken hearts and thinking of suicide. Then when their turn comes, they bound madly, organize a private cheering section, and go off whooping for dear old Siwash.

The basic equipment you need for Obedience Training is a chain collar, for cockers a lightweight length of meshed links like a girl's bracelet. The chain has two loops, one on either end, and you slip the chain through one loop, fasten the leash to the other. This is comfortable, easy to adjust, and enables you to guide or correct your angel by a slight jerk instead of a long haul on a heavy collar.

This is all you need for the novice work, for the first degree, which is Companion Dog.

All you need, that is, except a willingness to hike miles while the angel gets the idea of walking by your left side, with his shoulder parallel to your left ankle.

Now, whether or not you intend at this point to enter the shows, you should follow the regular Kennel Club rules for Obedience, because they are based on practical values.

There is not a single rule for the Obedience Work that is useless or just something for the dog to learn.

If you want to teach your dog to sit on a piano stool and paw at the ivories, that is your affair, and not mine. But what good does it do? It does not make music. It is not something that makes the dog respect himself or you. This applies to all the tricks—wearing sun glasses and reading a paper—you can make your own list. It offends the innate dignity of your dog and it does no service.

But take heeling. When you have a dog that heels, sits when you stop moving, and stays on command, just try going traveling. We took two C. D. cockers on a trip last winter. We wrote to the hotel and explained we were traveling with two Obedience trained dogs, and the hotel invited us to come along.

We walked across the lobby with Little Sister and Linda heeling modestly along. While we registered, they sat neatly and without a word. They rode the elevator without screaming.

By the time we left the hotel, the staff was all lined up to say good-bye and urge us to come back. And we had not worried when we went down to dinner. We laid their blanket on the bed and settled the girls down and told them to STAY.

I believe the ban on dogs in many hotels is based on unfortunate experiences the Management has had with unruly misbehaving dogs. And while I never will stay in a place nor eat at a restaurant (with or without my dogs) that discriminates against them, I can still see why some people do not want dogs around in public places.

In the advanced work, the rules still make sense.

For instance, scent discrimination—picking out metal, wood, or leather objects from a pile—think of the man and the auto keys.

And the dropping on signal might save a dog from being involved in a fight with a neighbor's bulldog, as I said before.

Just what must your dog do to qualify for the first degree? He must make a score of at least 170 out of a possible 200 in three shows under different judges. When he has done this, he is issued a certificate by the American Kennel Club, and is entitled to the letters C. D. after his name.

This is not easy. You will have Ginger performing perfectly and you will start off in high feather for your first show. You arrive. You push your way through hundreds of dogs and their humans.

"Where is the Obedience ring?" you ask a million times.

The Obedience ring is always the farthest off, in the hottest part of the field, and with the most noise going on around it. Obedience Work is still new enough to be viewed doubtfully by the breed show people. If possible, they put the ring where the cows have lately wandered, so the hunting dogs are absolutely bound to sniff and lose points. They put a loud speaker at the ring's edge, so a dog on the Long Sit will suddenly hear a shout braying, "Shepherd bitches in ring eleven!"

When you realize this, your hands grow clammy. The judge is late, you have plenty of time to worry. So does your pride and joy. Your friends arrive, and their dogs, and you all hang around an hour or so getting more and more nervous.

Finally the judge turns up and the stewards drift in.

Small boys appear like magic and swing on the ropes to the ring, pop paper bags of water, whistle, and throw stones at each other in the charming way of small boys in public. They never have any mammas, they are simply boys at a show.

You go in the ring. You see the judge dimly through a fog.

"Are you familiar with the rules?" he says, smiling a false smile.

Are you familiar with the rules? You have worked by them for months. They are engraved on the tablets of your brain—if you have any brain left.

"Forward," says the judge.

You stumble along, trying not to look down to see if your partner in this nightmare is heeling or just wandering idly along looking at the gallery. The next thing you know, you make a mistake yourself. You turn right instead of left. You give a double command. You walk too fast. You walk too slow. You run into the ropes.

When it is over, you fall on a bench and gulp a cup of coffee, and your friends tell you all the things you did wrong. Your heart slows in another hour or so, and you are ready to go in again for the Long Sit and the Long Down.

"And I just cannot see why you do it," says a non-doggy friend, "because you *suffer* so!"

And then, possibly, the judge calls your number and you run back into the ring. Your little candidate wags along beside you. You line up with three other dogs. You listen in a daze to the voice of the wonderful, wonderful judge saying that Cocker Spaniel number 72 out of a possible score of 200 has made 194 and a half. You gather in a ribbon, and a silver trophy or a bag of dog food, according to whether you are first or second.

Tired and dusty, but flushed with triumph, you lug your trophies and your picnic basket to the car and unsnap Dolly's leash. Your friends wave as they, too, get in their cars.

"See you at the show next week!" they call, as the fine dust rises behind the home-turning tires.

And you can hardly wait!

After the Companion Degree is safely tucked in your dog's paws, you work on the next stage, which is Companion Dog Excellent, known as C.D.X.

In the show, you are now in the Open Class, and the dumbbell has entered your life to stay.

The final degree is Utility Dog or U.D. and involves scent discrimination, among other things. And there is, in addition to these three regular degrees, the Tracking, which you may win at a special tracking test show.

STILLMEADOW HERITAGE TAKING THE BROAD JUMP

LINDA AND SISTER WITH DUMBBELLS

If you do not have a class to attend, you can get a good deal of help from special books on Obedience Work. Blanche Saunders, one of the pioneers in the field, has an excellent volume on training, with illustrations. *Training Your Spaniel*, by Paffenberger, is another. *Companion Dog Training*, by Tossutti, is a third. There are others, but these are very good.

You can learn from them the various steps in Obedience and how best to teach them. And from the American Kennel Club you can get the regulations for Obedience Work in shows.

The Gaines Research Center, at 250 Park Avenue, New York City, issues a good folder called *Every Dog A Gentleman*, which you may like to have.

If you have followed the directions in Chapter Ten for training your puppy, you already have a good start toward the regular Obedience Work. You also will have a faint idea of how much fun you and your dog can have together.

After a good many miles of going up and down the road in all sorts of weather, and a lot of evenings trotting around a gym floor, and many days taking the long trek to another show, and watching a good many trainers in classes, I naturally think of a lot of random ideas I have formed about my own cockers, cocker personality, and Obedience Training.

This is what I have learned, and wish I could

have read before I put the first collar on the first Stillmeadow Spaniel.

Never let a wrong habit become established. You know, for instance, that your dog should heel close to you. Not ahead looking for violets, not behind sniffing for a bone. He should not lean on you, nor heel half way across the road.

So, every single time you and your dog heel down the lane, *keep* him heeling correctly. Carry the leash loosely in your right hand, but give a jerk when he strays from the straight and narrow.

When he sits, have him sit *exactly* where he should every single time he sits at all. Never let him keep a half-crooked sit. Correct him at once.

And so on.

Correct your dog without anger, but with a firm tug on the training collar. And use the collar for correction, and *not your hand*.

Remember to praise him when he does well. How about you when you do something very nice? If nobody praises you, don't you feel like a forsaken soul yourself?

Cockers need praise as a rose needs water. And praise is enough without a tidbit. If you want to give a tidbit now and then, you may, but we use it only at the end of an exercise such as a Recall when it might help the dog to sit more correctly if he looks for that wafer. Little Sister does not like to be fed at all when she is working. But she runs to the cupboard afterward and looks up for her cookie.

Small dog biscuits or dog candy are good as a reward, and also inexpensive vanilla or arrowroot cookies.

A reward at the end of the work period ends the whole business on a happy social note.

Use the same words for the same commands always. I mention this because I have seen so many handlers confuse their dogs by careless speaking. When you say Heel, you mean Heel. Don't say, "Come on now, baby," the next time, and, "You behave yourself now, Rover," the time after.

Don't keep saying, "Bad dog," either and, "Wait until I get you home and see what happens." You hear women talking to their children that way sometimes and you are enraged. It is just as bad for your dog, because he doesn't even know what you are talking about.

The simple word No, repeated with firmness and solemnity, is the greatest help in correction.

Work always with a loose lead. Dragging your dog makes it impossible to correct him with a jerk, for he is already straining against the pull, and he will not enjoy any of it. In the ring, of course, it melts your score away.

Correct your dog on the spot where he makes the error, otherwise you are wasting your time and his.

Hazel Fletcher, one of the wisest trainers I

know, says that every dog is different, and you must understand the way *your own dog* thinks and then make your training program conform.

Don't overtrain your dog. You can wrap a wet towel around his head and make him study calculus all night, so to speak, and when you get the examination, he is just as apt to turn in a blank paper. What he learns when he is tired and bored with the whole thing is never going to stick in the long run.

Keep training yourself while you train your dog. On the Figure-eight exercise, be sure you don't walk so fast on that outer circle that the little cocker can't make it. On the About-turn, give him time to get all the way around you. Pivot slowly enough to accommodate to his speed.

Start with your left foot when you begin heeling. But if you are doing an exercise that requires him to stay behind you, such as the Long Sit or the Long Down, start with your right foot. He will quickly learn that the movement of your foot is an indication of the exercise.

Be sure your command is clearly heard before you begin the exercise. I learned this when I told Sister to Stay in the ring and walked away rapidly myself, and looked around to find Sister walking along just as rapidly beside me. I had not called the signals clearly enough.

You will soon learn that you and your dog are a team, and that you must always work together.

It is the destiny of a dog to be man's companion. There was that first dog that crept into the cave at the edge of the wilderness and offered his life to the caveman in return for a bone and the companionship of the man. They hunted together, for getting food was the major part of life in that time.

And now, in our so-called civilized world, the dog has come to share our complicated existence with the same willingness. All he expects is a little of our time to teach him the best things in this new life.

There is nothing much finer than to see a sturdy little cocker, eyes shining, tail whisking as he whips in for a perfect Recall. He is so proud of his education, so excited at your mutual achievement.

And as he sits before you, looking up, you look down into those dark and loving eyes.

You see the long walks in the twilight, the glaring lights of the training class, the muddy trails where the jumps stand. You see clear pale skies of spring, and darkened skies of autumn, and sifting bitter flakes of snow.

And you know suddenly how good it has all been. You feel as happy as it is ever given to a mortal to feel.

So, I'll see you in the Obedience ring!

32

I AM conscious of a deep sadness as I finish this. There are many omissions, since I am neither scientist nor veterinarian. I have felt it best to confine myself to matters I actually have first-hand experience with, therefore nothing is here that does not have its roots in my life with spaniels.

But the sadness comes not so much from this, as from a feeling that possibly somewhere there may be a dog-lover who is never able to own a dog. And if in these pages, I have given any impression that the care and training of dogs is a burden too ornerous to take on, it is a real tragedy.

The spaniels of Stillmeadow have told me many things, have taught me much. The practical, helpful tangible things I have been able to record for other spaniels and their owners. As the cockers race in and out of the room, lie dozing on the nearest couch, or climb up on the typewriting bench at hugging distance, they have made this their record.

But the one thing they have not been able to tell me is how immeasurably they have enriched my life. The intangible is not so easy to communicate, it is too much like sunset or apple blossoms in twilight or dark branches against a sky or fire on the hearth.

Surely that person is rare who never needs love and loyalty and warmth and selfless devotion in his life. That person does not need a dog. For the rest, unselfish love, patience in adversity, a cheerful spirit, unfailing approval, these are treasures in an unstable world well worth some small effort.

You will forever be young and beautiful to your dog, you will be wise, you will be marvelous, you are the main reason for existence. Whatever you do, you are never wrong, or petty or dull. There you are, you wonderful, heavenly being, you fragment of divinity on earth!

How empty a house is without a dog, or better still, dogs. It is like a defrosting refrigerator; even the light is out. No dog hairs on the rug, no chewed books, no old bones under your pillow, and nobody flying around, tail whipping, ears swinging, eyes shining. No small soft body flinging itself into your arms, no wet tongue sandpapering your face, no gusty breath of excitement blown down your neck.

This is a pretty grave world, and it's a fine thing that there is a recipe for happiness which you may buy for the price of an extra coat.

Town or country, train or car, afoot or horseback, the dog doesn't care. Just so he is your companion, basking in the radiance of your presence.

I like to stand in the yard under the old apple

trees at sunset and watch the Stillmeadow spaniels saying good-bye to day. Golden puppies tearing a lawn chair to pieces, a dark red warrior nose deep in a mole hole, a shy dark girl nosing at the edge of the deep grass, two black and whites racing back and forth along the picket fence as the neighbor's cows move dreamily toward the barn.

And a couple of spaniels at my feet, looking up with soft dark eyes. "Now what are you thinking of?" they ask.

"Thinking about dogs," I answer, "especially spaniels".

Index

INDEX

Abscesses, 157
Accidents, general, 160–162
American Kennel Club, 18, 19, 108, 180, 186, 190, 193

Bathing, 105, 106, 136
Bedding, 39, 40, 127, 136, 142
Boils, 157
Bones, broken, 162
Bowels, 46, 157
Breeding, general, 17, 19, 84, 86, 89
    for color, 79–81
    stud, choice of, 78, 79
        cost of, 79
        fee, 36
    time, 82, 86
Burns, 162
Buying your dog, 16, 32–34

Characteristics, 22–24, 33, 78, 79
Chorea, 124, 152, 176
Constipation, 87, 137, 138
Cracked or cut pads, 161

Dandruff, 141
Degrees, Companion Dog, 185, 188, 190, 192
    Companion Dog Excellent, 192
    Utility Dog, 192
    Tracking, 192
Diarrhea, 124, 126, 127, 156
Diet, 55, 58–63, 86, 98, 103, 141, 174
    10 weeks to 6 months, 56

203

  6 months to 10 months, 57
  reinforcements, 60
Distemper, 13, 124, 131, 140, 176
  symptoms, 123, 129, 130, 151
  inoculation, 123, 125
  cure of, 126, 127
Dog Shows, 107, 111, 180
  classes, 109
  entry blanks, 108
  posing, 112
  preparation, 110, 111
  prizes and awards, 110
Douche, 84

Ear canker, 117
  mites, 117, 118
Ears, care of, 116, 117
Eclampsia, 99, 129, 146–149
Eczema, 140, 141
Enemas, 137, 138
Environment, 172
Eyes, care of, 121, 122

Females, breeding time, 82, 86
  in season, symptoms, 24–29
  spaying, 26
Fits, 150, 151, 176
Fleas, 119, 120
Formula, weaning, 102
  whelping, supplementary, 96

Grooming, 118, 169

Health hints, general, 116, 173
Heating, 40, 41
Housebreaking, 45–47, 49, 52, 54

Irrigation, 64

Laxatives, 86, 122, 138

Males, in season, 29, 30
Mange, 140, 142
Medicine cabinet list, 168, 169

Nursing, 101

Obedience, degree, 75, 180, 185, 186, 188, 190, 192
    ring, 75
    trial, 74, 180
    work, 75, 179–183, 187, 188, 190, 193
Obstructions, intestines, 137
    throat, 162

Personality problems, 171, 176
    traits, 183
Poison, 154
    food, 156
    toxic, 156
Porcupine quills, removal of, 161
Puppies, care of, 92, 93
    bathing, 105, 106, 136
    formula, 56, 57, 102
    tail-cutting, 94
    weaning, 101–103

Rabies, 158, 159
Registration fee, individual, 19
    litter, 19, 109
Ringworm, 140, 142–145

Sedatives, 127
    list of, 152, 153
Sickness, general, 115
Skin diseases, general, 119, 140

Spaying, 26
Sterility, 85
Strain, 161

Tail-cutting, 94
Teeth, care of, 122
Temperature, 128–130
Tendons, pulled, 161
Ticks, 119, 121
Training, general, 75, 178, 182, 187, 193, 196
    heeling, 67, 71, 187, 189, 194, 195
    retrieving, 72, 74
    sitting, 68, 71, 185, 190, 192, 194
    walking on leash, 65–67, 69, 70, 194

Weaning, 101–103
Whelping, box, 87
    formula, supplementary feeding, 96
    kit, 88
    labor, 91
    postnatal care, 92, 93, 98, 101
    prenatal care, 86, 87, 131
Worms, 55, 86, 131–136, 140, 174
Wounds, 161